OVERCOMING CHILDHOOD ADVANTAGES

OVERCOMING CHILDHOOD ADVANTAGES

Rosalie Dwyer

REGENT PRESS
BERKELEY, CALIFORNIA

Copyright 2011 © Rosalie Dwyer
ALL RIGHTS RESERVED

ISBN 13: 978-1-58790-219-2
ISBN 10: 1-58790-219-2
Library of Congress Control Number: 2011925139

Manufactured in the U.S.A.
REGENT PRESS
2747 Regent Street
Berkeley, California
www.regentpress.net

Contents

I. Childhood and Teens
Overcoming Childhood Advantages — 3
The Big Shack — 8
Homeground — 14
Important People:
    Gargo — 20
    Helena — 28
    WTS — 35
    Granny Plans — 42
Dr. Kubler Ross, Meet Dr. Kevorkian — 47
Home Entertainment — 52
Christmas Time — 57
More Celebrations — 63
Early Crimes — 68
Early Music — 72
Summer Fun:
    Camp Fire Camp — 76
    The Ranch — 82
    Carmel by the Sea — 86
    Mt. Hamilton — 91
Public Appearances — 95
The Road to Wellness — 100
Awareness of Sex — 104
The Opposite Sex — 107
Love Notes — 111
People Don't Like You for Your I.Q. — 113
Junior High Daze — 116

Summer Romance — 125
Cal — 131
Lying for Love — 141

II. Marriage and Other New Experiences, 1953-1989

Army Bride I — 147
Army Bride II — 153
First Pregnancy — 158
Baby Makes Three — 164
Starting Civilian Life — 172
Salinas — 176
Back to Berkeley / Loosening the Mold — 180
A Change of Scene (Overton) — 187
Transitions — 191
Feather River Summer — 196
Back to the Land (Petaca) — 202
First Grandchild — 209
A Season of Change — 215
Dropping Out - With A Safety Net, 1975 — 221
A Weekend at Esalen — 227
Trailer Travels and Travails — 233
Suburban Crime — 240
At the Bottom of the Grand Canyon — 245
Do-It-Yourself Vision Quest — 251
Getting to Alaska — 254
Encounter at the Boarder — 260
Singing For the Soviets — 265
A Hostel Environment — 270
A Spiritual Autobiography — 275

I

Childhood and Teens

My parents, Walter and Elizabeth Steillberg, in their eighties.

My female triumverate: Great grandmother Elizabeth von Everen; Mother Elizabeth; Grandmother Mary Effie Fergerson. Circa 1916.

Overcoming Childhood Advantages

I spent the first 20 years of my life in Berkeley, California, in a beautiful home designed by my architect father in the hills overlooking all of San Francisco Bay and right next door to the University of California campus. Before my birth, my mother was research assistant to a famous botanist who was also our next door neighbor. My maternal grandmother, who lived with us, had attended Cornell University but family illness had prevented her from graduating, and this lack made her feel inferior to her brother and sister, both of whom were successful professionals back East. My half-sister, six years older than I, was talented both musically and artistically and attended schools in Switzerland and Germany until the Depression curtailed family finance. My grandmother traveled abroad extensively, both as chaperone for my sister and on worldwide expeditions of her own. When I was three-and-a-half our whole family went to Europe for six months and I was dragged through every museum, cathedral, palace, architectural wonder and ruin in France, Italy and Germany. Back home, I was taken to concerts, plays, art exhibits, dance recitals and, occasionally, the San Francisco Zoo.

Thus my early years were spent immersed in a cultural stew, which was often too rich for me to digest. Our home was filled with fine Oriental rugs, uncomfortable Chinese teak furniture, Asian and European art objects, and mementos of everyone's travels. Many supper-table conversations were reminiscences of trips abroad, and since I was the only family member who couldn't remember our European tour, I often felt left out. The classical music we listened to ("Remember that performance at the Salzburg Festival, La Scala or wherever?"); the games we played (rummy sets of famous artists, composers or authors in German, French and Italian); and the songs we sang (Christmas carols in German, folk songs in French) were things I could enjoy at the time but not much use away from home. I even got my sister to teach me some German swear words but didn't know on whom to use them. My parents' friends were professors of science or philosophy, artists, musicians, architects and writers, and their conversation was all in the language of Enlightened Liberals.

I started kindergarten at a small private school and was immediately put in the first grade because I could already read, resulting in more feelings of my being "different." The following year the market crashed and I had to be transferred to public school, the first child on my mother's side of the family to be subjected to this supposedly inferior sort of education. My mother and grandmother were Quakers, whose tradition regarding the importance of education for both sexes went back for many generations and resulted in their own fine schools. (In 1840, my great, great-grandmother was principal of a Quaker high school which taught girls algebra and Latin.) At this time (1929) my sister was still going to school abroad and my mother seemed really worried and apologetic that I was to be sacrificed to the rigid and stultifying public school system.

No one was hiring residential architects in those years; my mother switched her career to social worker and got a job with Alameda County Welfare as a caseworker. We rented rooms in our large home to University teachers and workers who were still getting salaries, however small. My grandmother made budget meals. I particularly disliked the tamale pie and something made with hominy and canned tomatoes, and she made most of my clothes; bulky, unfashionable sweaters and skirts with drooping hemlines. Gone were the cute frocks from the City of Paris. When my sister returned from Munich in 1932, we had to share a room, which I'm sure bothered her more than it did me. I heard a lot of talk about how poor we were, but I certainly did not suffer during the Depression. In later years, when my contemporaries started telling their woeful tales of deprivation and sacrifice during those times, I actually felt ashamed and embarrassed that I had been so fortunate.

I learned some things in public school though probably not what my parents wanted me to learn. I knew how to talk so as to sound more like the other children; how to keep quiet when I knew the answer so the other kids wouldn't think I was a show-off; how to give a teacher what she wanted so I could get an "A". By high school I had learned to act and dress pretty much like my peers, though this entailed a huge struggle at home: "Why do you want to be just like everyone else?" I didn't know why, I just knew that was exactly the way I wanted to be. I got up the courage to stop piano lessons after 10 years. I learned to curl my hair and to put on lipstick on the way to the streetcar. I dared to listen to popular music instead of the classical fare I had been fed since babyhood. Everything from Billie Holiday and Duke Ellington to Frank Sinatra and Tommy Dorsey seemed wonderful to me. I read True Confessions and Redbook instead of more Dickens or Kipling. But I still did not know the meaning of the two most commonly used four-letter words (which I had seen chalked on the sidewalk) and my grandmother was of no help in enlightening me. (My mother and sister must have been away at the time.) When I graduated from high school, before my sixteenth birthday, I had never had a date, through I had been kissed once by the minister's son, an experience I didn't find worth repeating.

OVERCOMING CHILDHOOD ADVANTAGES

I grew up being told that I was specially privileged to be part of a family like mine in a town as progressive as Berkeley — far ahead of the rest of the country. I could do or be anything I wanted to — preferably an M.D. or a PhD. — but I didn't quite live up to expectations. I did well in college, finished PreMed, PreNursing, a semester of UC Nursing School and finally a major in Biology in my four-year course, but I didn't make Phi Beta Kappa like my mother and sister. And I had fallen in love when I was 16 with the man who was to be my husband for life. We were married on my 20th birthday, just two months after I graduated from Cal.

So I left Berkeley and my ivory tower to be a Second Lieutenant's wife in a rundown vacation cabin near Fort Lewis, Washington. I still felt and looked like a schoolgirl, but the three other Second Lieutenants' wives who were my neighbors hadn't even been to college, never heard of Berkeley and couldn't care less. They knew about pleasing their husbands (even though bad-mouthing them to each other) and how to deal with them when they got drunk and argumentative. They knew how to play poker and bridge, how to mix drinks of many kinds, how to make celery curls and radish rosettes, how to style hair and apply makeup, and how to keep house on very little money. From them I learned how to sew curtains by hand and how to make a ruffled cover to turn an Army footlocker into a coffee table. They were my first teachers in the wide world outside Berkeley. I have had many more teachers since, in places as different as Salinas, San Pedro, Sacramento, Gardena, Point Reyes, Santa Cruz and Overton, Nevada. For more than 50 years I tried to counteract the effects of my overly intellectual, genteel and protected upbringing. I learned to talk dirty, dress sloppy, be practically unshockable, pay attention to pop culture and New Age trends and rarely mention the superiority of Berkeley.

I was gone from Berkeley for 59 years, though I visited frequently because my parents were alive until the 70's and my two older children still live here, as well as 3 grandchildren. Four years ago, as my mobility problems grew more limiting, I returned here after 25 years in Aptos. My husband had died in 1989, very suddenly from heart failure, and I needed more family nearby. I cannot live in my pink ivory tower because climbing the 50 or 60 stairs to it is too difficult due to the pain and weakness of spinal arthritis and myasthenia gravis (a muscle wasting affliction), so I live in a small, comfy bungalow in the proletarian flatlands. But, again, I am enjoying concerts, art exhibits, museums, plays and great architecture, as well as my family.

The Big Shack

The Ivory Tower where I spent the first 20 years of my life was, in reality, made of redwood, pink stucco and glass. It was octagonal in shape and rose up three-and-a-half stories from the Berkeley hillside, overlooking the UC Campus and all of San Francisco Bay. It was the center and the landmark feature of the home my father designed for my mother, grandmother and great grandmother. Then he and my mother fell in love and it became his home, too. Sometime, over the years, the grandchildren began calling it, affectionately, The Big Shack — perhaps to distinguish it from the two smaller houses on the property.

The house was (and is) beautiful, imaginative, lovingly crafted and created to make the most of the dramatic view. The first floor of the tower, above the basement and flanked by the living room, pantry and kitchen, was the dining room. Here, six of the eight sides were windows or French doors, with a fireplace on the seventh side and mirrored doors on the eighth, so that no matter where one sat one had a magnificent view of the Bay and the Golden Gate. The French doors of the north and south octants led out onto terraces in the garden, the one on the south being shaded by a large wisteria vine which let down its lovely lavender clusters every spring. To the west, the doors opened onto a small wrought-iron balcony, shaded by an almond tree. The balcony was just big enough for me to sleep on when I wanted to be outside but close to the house on a summer night.

The dining room itself had a round table and six chairs, all of woven wicker, which, as they aged, proved to be dangerous for knit shirts and silk stockings. The andirons in the fireplace were long black dachshunds, which later disappeared with a tenant. My father loved Chinese art and decor so the side tables were heavy, dark teak merchant's desks, to match the living room furniture, and a large Chinese lantern hung over the dining table. The table could hold only six people, but when my parents had dinner parties, a huge, round plywood tabletop, which was hinged in the middle and stored, folded in half, in the laundry room, was hauled out and put on top of the smaller table. It could easily accommodate 12, but you had to be careful not to lean too hard on the side of it. Often there would be a small "Kindertisch" or children's table (as my grandmother liked to call it) for me and my sister and any other children present. Under the wickerwork table was a buzzer to step on to summon a maid, but we usually had serving help only on special occasions. One of my few household tasks was setting the table, and I remember how proud I felt when I was considered old enough to set the big table for parties.

The second floor of the tower was a bedroom often assigned to me, though it was one of four on that floor and I slept in each of them at different times. The surrounding bedrooms and hall, except for the front three eighths where big windows opened out to the same grand view of the Bay, obscured the octagon shape. The window coverings were apple green, wooden Venetian blinds, whose color matched all the trim on the house.

My bed was of blond Philippine mahogany, one of six which my father had had made for the family. Unfortunately, they were only six feet long — long enough for the original users but, when my tall husband joined the family, he had to hang his heels over the end. (As our children and grandchildren grew up, several of them grew too long for the beds, also.)

OVERCOMING CHILDHOOD ADVANTAGES

Until I was in junior high school, I was sent to bed very early, about 7:30 p.m. I liked to lie in my bed by the west-facing window in the evening twilight and listen to the birds' goodnight calls from the almond trees, then watch the lights come on all over the city and across the Bay. I especially liked the neon ad signs and my favorite of these was the Sherwin Williams Paint Company one, down by the waterfront. It showed a can repeatedly tipping and pouring red paint over a crosshatched globe to illustrate the slogan, "We cover the earth." I could hear the sound of the train whistles down at Berkeley Station and, occasionally, from Telegraph Avenue, 7 long blocks away, I heard newsboys crying, "Extra! Extra!"

The campanile on campus chimed every hour, day and night. During the day, two sides of the face were visible from my tower bedroom, but sometimes the times didn't agree! The carillon was played for 10 minutes before 8 a.m., noon, and 6 p.m. by a tiny, energetic woman named Margaret Murdoch. She was an excellent musician and on Sundays she gave half-hour mid-afternoon concerts; there was special music for Christmas, Easter and other holidays, too. I loved the sound of the bells and no set of bells I've heard since sounds nearly as sweet.

The top floor of the tower was my favorite room. It was originally designed to be open on seven sides and had a heavy canvas floor and a sturdy redwood railing set with the green Chinese tiles, which were one of my father's trademarks. But Berkeley weather is often damp or windy and soon the room was enclosed with seven double French doors, the eighth wall being the mirrored door to the hall. Another enclosed sun porch, my father's study and darkroom and the attic comprised the rest of the top floor. In the hall was a built-in speaking/whistling tube, with openings on both lower floors so that members of the family could be summoned to meals, phone calls or other events. It was a great way for children to communicate!

The view from the top of the tower was truly breathtaking, from one end of the Bay to the other with the Golden Gate directly opposite. The room was above the tops of the almond trees, the chestnut, the acacia, and the plums, and on a level with the tops of the tall poplars, which lined the approach to the house. On very clear days, we could see the Farallon Islands, 40 miles out to sea. We knew that the sun always set in the Golden Gate during February and October. This glass room was my playroom and often, also, my bedroom — with or without my sister as roommate. It was a place where I could escape from adult supervision and enter my fantasy world. The attic had several trunks full of once elegant dresses and hats, which my grandmother had brought west in 1914 when she and her mother and daughter moved to California from New York State. My friends and I were allowed to dress up in these costumes and pretend to be grand ladies. I also kept my large family of dolls in this tower room and played with them until I was almost twelve, an addiction that caused my mother to worry about me. After all, I was in junior high school! But I was frequently the only child in a family of adults, for my sister spent several years at schools in Switzerland and Germany, then entered the young adult world at UC Berkeley when she was 16. I really needed my dolls to have someone to boss around, to give me a sense of control in a world of powerful grown-ups.

Sleeping in the glass tower had advantages and disadvantages. I was far enough from the rest of the family to feel some independence and could read till late at night. Of course, I had to read under the covers by flashlight because any exposed light would shine out those windows like a beacon to alert my guardians in the living room two floors down. The disadvantage was that being far away could be scary. When the wind blew, branches scraped the glass and all the French doors shook and rattled. Sometimes cats or squirrels on the roof would make strange noises in the night. I think I was seven when the Lindbergh baby was kidnapped and murdered. I lay awake a lot of nights wondering if anyone wanted to kidnap me and if there were ladders long enough to reach all the way up to the top of the tower.

The part of the tower I didn't like was the basement, part of which was dug into the hillside, so it was dark and airless down there. This was also the furnace room where racks of laundry were dried in wet weather. Narrow, steep, curving concrete stairs led down to it from the main hall and sometimes I would be asked to go down and see if the clothes were dry. I was afraid of the furnace. It was enormous, with long fat ducts looming up like threatening arms and the gas made a roaring noise. When I was about four years old there had been a terrible explosion north of the Campus, caused by a home gas furnace. One of my parents' friends and his daughter were killed. For years, I would go open the door to the basement every time the furnace was turned on, so I could listen and be sure it really had lit.

The Big Shack belongs to me now — and to my children after me. When my parents died, my sister didn't want the headaches of property management, so she sold me her share. A long procession of tenants has moved in and out, mostly students and University workers. An eighty-nine year old house requires a lot of maintenance and repair. The place has been re-roofed and rewired to accommodate microwave ovens, electric heaters, extra refrigerators and a coin-op washer and dryer in the laundry room. There are now shower heads in all four bathtubs; people are too busy to take tub baths these days. All the outside doors, which we never locked except at night, are now kept locked and bolted at all times because of repeated thefts.

My older daughter lives on the top floor and oversees all the problems. She keeps the yard looking lovely. The almonds, plums, chestnut and acacia tree are all long gone but other trees have taken their places and the oak seedlings have grown higher than the top of the tower. The wisteria still bloom profusely over the dining room terrace and the pergola. The tenants do the cleaning, even polishing the hardwood floors occasionally; they put up with leaks, plumbing breakdowns, repainting and other inconveniences, such as no parking spots. They seem to feel very lucky to live in the place, which, a few years ago, was listed as a California Historical Landmark.

Many treasures had to be disposed of when my parents died. The Chinese art and furnishings — the heavy, dark, carved teak furniture, the Chinese scrolls and lanterns and porcelain figurines, the fine pewter and cloisonné vases, the wicker furniture and the lovely Chinese dishes we ate from are gone. Gone, also, are the grand piano, the fine silver, the hundreds of books and *National Geographics,* the antique clocks, the Venetian blinds, the steamer trunks in the attic, the Oriental and Navajo rugs and the mementos from world travels. Everything was sold or allotted to family members. The mahogany beds are stored in the attic since most young people like to sleep on the floor these days. But the tower and the view are still there and they are really the only things I miss when living elsewhere.

Homeground

The Big Shack is what my children call the house I grew up in but it is only a part of my family's Berkeley property. Below it, on the same large lot, is The Cottage, a charming three room redwood building, over a double garage. This is where my mother and father spent the first months of their married life while they waited for the big house to be finished. After that, it was usually rented — for a while to me and Ed and our two small children during the time he went back to Cal to get his Master's. It was designed by my father for one or two people, with a large living room, a tiny kitchen, and a very small bedroom which was also the passageway to the garden, so fitting all four of us into it was a challenge.

Running from the back of the cottage for about 50 feet, parallel to the street and one terrace above it, is the pergola. It is brick-paved with a trellis top covered, in spring and summer, with white wisteria and climbing pink roses. When I was a child, I could nail boards across the slats on top, to make a fragrant, sunny hideaway. The pergola itself had room for a swing, rings, trapeze and seesaw, which provided a lot of fun for me and visiting children.

At the far end of the Pergola is the Playhouse, a one room redwood cottage with leaded amber windows to insure privacy from the people passing on the sidewalk below. The croquet, badminton and archery sets were stored here as well as my scooter and bicycle and other outdoor toys. It was our dressing room when my sister presented her version of various plays to family and neighbors gathered on the lawn above. I remember playing minor parts in *Bluebeard* and *A Midsummer Night's Dream* when I was five or six and my sister and her friends were eleven or twelve. Sometimes I would sleep overnight in the playhouse, with or without a friend. For such occasions we had canvas Army cots that pinched one's fingers when being assembled and sleeping bags of kapok lined with lambs wool. My mother and grandmother belonged to the Sierra Club and, starting in 1914, had been on a number of their High Trips. The playhouse had electricity but it was damp and sometimes mold grew on the brick floor.

Up one terrace from the pergola was the large lawn where we played croquet and badminton, practiced archery, did gymnastics and dancing and ran through the sprinklers in the summer. A plum tree overhung the lawn and dropped its sweet fruit every summer, attracting many honeybees. We had to be very careful when going barefoot there. The property had been an almond orchard and there were still several large almond trees around the lawn, good for climbing. I loved to pick and eat the almonds, cracking open their fuzzy green shells to get at the nuts. Before they were ripe, the centers were a delicious clear jelly, which I liked as much as the mature nut. Of course, there were many noisy blue jays competing with me. In the mornings, lying in bed, I could hear them cracking the nuts on the roof.

At one end of the lawn was the crab-apple tree, which I could climb to get on the playhouse roof. It was another of my hiding places, among the fragrant blossoms. Every August I helped pick the crab-apples so my grandmother could make jelly. The cooked pulp hung in a cheesecloth bag over a big kettle set in the laundry tub, where it slowly dripped its juice. Sometimes I was allowed to gently squeeze this bag to hurry the straining; I loved the way it felt! As I grew older I was allowed to pour the melted paraffin on top of the finished jars of jelly. I always sneaked some extra paraffin for chewing gum, of which my family disapproved. Gum-chewing was uncouth and looked "like a cow chewing her cud."

Under the living room terrace was an arched grotto of ferns and moss and the goldfish pond. We had fish there sporadically but the cats usually got them. One time my father braved a rabid dog at the pond and kept it corralled until the Pound could come for it. I was frightened and impressed, never having thought of my father as brave before. In any contest of wills with my mother or grandmother, he usually lost.

My mother was a botanist when she married, and my father built her a greenhouse at the back of the property above the big house. It was torn down in 1932, by which time my mother had become a social worker, and replaced by an all-concrete house (my father's innovative earthquake proof design, highly appropriate for a building sitting on top of the Hayward Fault!) This house provided us with rental income during the Depression, and still does. But I remember the greenhouse fondly as a warm, moist place with a mysterious green light — another retreat for me when life got too complicated.

Keeping a place this size running smoothly required help, and we had it. My mother and grandmother did most of the gardening but there was a Japanese man — or a series of them — who did lawn mowing, raking, trimming and pruning. My grandmother ran the house as my mother was working and was not very domestic, anyway. The first household helper I remember was Mrs. Ramsbottom. My sister and I had a lot of fun with her name, but she was a no-nonsense person. She cleaned, washed dishes, did laundry and some cooking and rarely smiled or talked. We got much better acquainted with Miss Daisy Nolan who came weekly to iron, do mending and wash our hair. She washed it with tan Castile soap and rinsed it with lemon juice, which really stung if it got in your eyes. My mother and grandmother both had waist length hair, which my mother braided and wound around her head in a coronet and my grandmother twisted up in a plain, sensible knot. If it were a sunny day my mother, who was very beautiful, would go sit on the lawn to dry her hair. I would watch her running her tortoiseshell comb through the long brown ripples in a way that made me think of the siren Lorelei.

One time I came home from school and found Miss Nolan ironing in the laundry room. I liked to visit with her, especially if no one else was home. But this time her face looked terrible, sunken in and puckered. "What happened to you?" I asked. "A horse kicked me in the mouth," she replied. When I reported this to my grandmother later, she explained to me about tooth extraction and false teeth — something I'd never heard of.

There was also Mr. Matsumoto who came every six weeks or so to clean and polish the Philippine mahogany floors. Whenever I smell kerosene or floor wax I can still see him on his hands and knees, working his way backwards. The cry, "Mr. Matsumoto's in the dining room," (living room, hall, stairs, etc.) meant we had to stay out of that part of the house until the buffing was done. I was glad I didn't have his job; it looked like a backbreaker.

We depended on other helpers, too: the milkman who came daily, the glass bottles clinking in his wire carrier; the iceman who had to carry his big cakes up at least 100 feet of steep, narrow stairs (He often gave me little slivers of ice to suck and crunch.); the garbage man who had to carry his burden down the same stairs; the postman who came twice a day and who was invited in for coffee on foggy mornings or lemonade on hot afternoons; the grocery delivery boy who brought most of our meat and staples. Fruits and vegetables were gotten

OVERCOMING CHILDHOOD ADVANTAGES

from the Chinese vegetable man whose truck came up the hill almost every weekday. His horn made a distinctive sound so people knew when he had arrived and went down to the street to buy. There were some strange looking vegetables hanging from the sides of his truck but my grandmother purchased only familiar ones.

Gargo, which was my grandmother's nickname, did almost all the cooking for our family of five. The kitchen was her domain and I liked to watch her working there and help her when she let me. There was a big gas stove, double porcelain sinks with wooden drain boards, a dishwasher (a real innovation in the 1920's!), the icebox, which drained directly to the ground through a hole in the floor, and a cooler cupboard which opened to the outside, where food not requiring refrigeration was kept on wire shelves. The cooler was plagued with ants so we put little dishes of water under each of its feet to keep the pests from crawling upward. We also used ant sticks and no one seemed to worry about the presence of arsenic in the kitchen.

Gargo wasn't really a very good cook. She knew about vitamins and nutrition but she tended to overcook everything and used almost no seasoning. What she was good at was making cookies, cakes — especially gingerbread — and candy. I always got to lick the mixing bowl. There was a large marble slab on one kitchen counter, for rolling out pie dough or cooling taffy or fudge. Taffy pulls were a favorite treat if I had friends over, but they could get pretty messy.

When it was suppertime and I had the table all set I got to call the rest of the family to eat, sometimes with the speaking tube but usually with a pretty little brass bell, made in the shape of a long-skirted woman (Dutch? Belgian?) with long braids and a cap. I really liked summoning the rest of the family that way. But the nicest way for our family to get each others attention was with our family whistle of seven notes: C-B-C-

D-C-A-F, ending on the descending triad, which we all recognized wherever we were. I couldn't whistle till I was about six but it was a wonderful way to signal to another family member, anywhere in the house or the yard, on the street or on a hike. Many times it saved me from being lost in a crowd.

Important People
Gargo

My mother's mother, Mary Effie Van Everen Ferguson, was my only living grandparent. Her nickname, Gargo, was supposed to have been derived from my baby talk for grandmother. Though the name was spelled with an "r" it was pronounced Gahgo by family members because that was the way my mother and grandmother talked.

Mary Effie grew up in Upstate New York, the middle child of a Quaker family whose ancestors had come to this country from England in 1636 and who had prospered here. Quaker tradition puts a high value on equal rights and education for women. One of our female forebears was the principal of a Friends' School for girls, which taught Latin and Algebra — in 1840! Effie, as she was called then, had an older brother who attended Harvard and became a successful patent attorney in Boston. Her younger sister went to MIT and became a microbiologist for the State of New York but died of cancer when she was only thirty-one. Effie went to Cornell University for a while, studying Montessori teachings, but as the older daughter she was called upon to cope with family illnesses and problems and she never graduated. Because of this she always felt educationally inferior to her siblings.

She was married at twenty-five to a second-cousin who was not the man she pined for. That man had married someone else. She produced my mother, her only child, but within two years of that event, she was forced to put her husband in a mental institution for her own and her child's safety. His family probably never forgave her for that but the disease was incurable, and he died in the hospital when my mother was four.

Fortunately, Effie had some money of her own, which her business wise father must have invested for her. She and my mother went to live in the family home again and she resumed her role as family helper. That same year, 1900, her sister Abby's son was born and Effie had a good deal to do with raising him, especially after Abby became fatally ill. (She died in 1905.) In 1908, Effie's much loved father died suddenly of a heart attack. Now her mother, who was in frail health, was Effie's responsibility. The two women and the young girl, my mother, spent a few winters in Florida for great-grandmother's health and then a winter in Pasadena, California, where there was a Quaker colony. They liked Pasadena so much that they returned with all their possessions and my mother finished Friends' High School there. When she went on to the University at Berkeley, all three women moved there and decided to settle.

After my mother's college graduation, while she was working as a botanist for one of her professors and studying for a Master's Degree, Effie decided that it was time to build a home for her three-woman household. Apparently, she had accumulated enough from her inheritance and investments to do it in style. She hired a young architect who lived nearby and whose work she had seen and admired. He was a widower with a small daughter. She didn't realize that within a year or so, he would be her son-in-law and, later, my father.

The big, beautiful house that my father designed was not yet finished when he and my mother were married. They lived, with my half sister, in the small cottage on the same property, while Gargo and her mother stayed on in the nearby apartment they had been renting. When the big house was ready for occupancy, I believe Gargo offered halfheartedly to live elsewhere with her mother. My father would not hear of such a thing;

the house had been designed for the three women and he was an interloper! My mother agreed with him, though I think secretly she would have preferred to be free of the female troika at last. Had that happened, my life and my mother's would have been completely different.

Gargo had raised my mother to become the professional woman that she, herself, had been prevented from being because of family commitments. Nothing was more important than that my mother graduate from college with honors and pursue her chosen field, which was Botany. Consequently, I don't think my mother had to do any of the household tasks Gargo was so good at. Hired help was cheap and easy to find, so I doubt if my mother knew how to iron, clean house or cook anything except the most basic fare. I never saw her sewing or darning except when my father asked her to sew a button on his shirt, occasionally, and that was pretty much of a token role-acknowledgment. When my mother acquiesced to Gargo in the running of the household, it meant she never really had to learn domestic skills because Gargo was good at all of them, or thought she was. There was usually someone to do the cleaning and ironing, including running the mangle, which pressed all the sheets and linens. But Gargo did everything else — cooking, baking, sewing, knitting, making dresses and curtains, dyeing material to get the colors she wanted. She could rewire electric lights and make simple repairs to plumbing and woodwork, tasks my father was no good at. She did a lot of the gardening, ordered the groceries or walked to the market, and generally ran the show. If my mother had ideas of her own there was usually a noisy argument, which ended in tears and slammed doors. It was not a peaceful household.

Gargo was sometimes away for long periods, traveling on her own or staying with my sister while she was at school in Europe. Then my mother cooked, never anything fancy like candy, cake or cookies, or we went out to eat — often to The Black Sheep on Telegraph Avenue. Hired help did the other chores. I missed Gargo when she was away but there were a lot fewer fights.

My mother worked and studied at the University when I was small, switching from botany to psychology. When the Depression hit and my father had no work, she went to work as a social worker for the County Welfare Department. I was seven then, and Gargo became more important than ever in my life. She was there, with cookies and milk, when I came home from school. She made my lunches, came to school affairs, oversaw my piano practice, took me shopping for clothes and shoes, and to see the doctor or dentist. When I was home sick she brought me trays and medicines and treatments and read to me or played games with me. (If I was sick enough to stay home from school I was also supposed to stay in bed.)

Gargo was my mainstay but she was also a source of ridicule for my sister and me. And she could be very intimidating with her strict Victorian beliefs about behavior, causing us to stretch the truth for self-protection. We had to get up early, get dressed and make our beds before we came down to breakfast, be quiet when adults were speaking, never walk in front of an adult, never talk back, sit in a ladylike fashion (feet on floor, knees together), rise when adult visitors entered the room and remain standing until they were comfortably seated, always ask permission to leave the room, always say "Please" and "Thank You" and play quietly when indoors.

Maybe that last injunction helped to develop my great love of the outdoors where I was pretty much unsupervised. My mother tended to be more lenient, especially after she started studying child psychology, and I was often guilty of asking her permission to do something which Gargo had already forbidden — go to a friend's house, stay up later, have dessert when

OVERCOMING CHILDHOOD ADVANTAGES

I hadn't finished my supper, or whatever bending of the rules I was after. But these differences of opinion on child-rearing could lead to more noisy and frightening scenes as my two "mothers" fought it out over me. (My father took no part in my discipline. He knew when to make himself scarce.) Gargo usually lost and would retreat to her room, stomping up the stairs in tears and slamming doors after herself. My sister and I tried to handle these scenes by making a joke of them or just disappearing, but we also learned how to avoid confrontation and how to be peacemakers. Often the same sort of tantrums started at the table when Gargo felt her cooking was unappreciated. I'm not surprised that I developed a perennially uneasy digestion. Of course, Gargo had a delicate digestion, too, which I could have inherited physically or psychologically.

The thing about Gargo we thought was ridiculous was her underwear. We knew that, underneath her prim cotton shirtwaist house dresses or the knit suits and classic silky frocks she wore for dressy occasions, she always wore a knit rayon undershirt and knee length bloomers and a corset which had lots of stays and laces in it. She was tall for those days, 5 feet, 9 inches, rather flat chested and not at all fat, and it was a mystery why she wore that uncomfortable garment every day of her life. Perhaps she thought it was the only way to hold up her long, orangey tan stockings, thick cotton for everyday, silk for dress. Her shoes were always sensible, low heeled, well laced and expensive. Her hats were funny, too. They were really pretty conservative, straw or felt according to the season, with high crowns and medium wide brims. But she never went anywhere without putting on a hat and coat or jacket and usually gloves. We girls knew a lot of older adults did this, but we didn't see the point of it in Berkeley. Gargo's long, grey hair was twisted into a rope and piled on top of her head with the aid of many tortoise shell combs and hairpins. Maybe the hats were to preserve this arrangement when she went out in the elements.

Gargo was by no means "just a homemaker." She traveled, often alone, all over Europe, India, the Middle and Far East and elsewhere. She read widely, everything from Lin Yutang to current political and social pundits, historians, naturalists and earlyday conservationists like John Muir and Joseph Wood Krutch. She was especially fond of Mark Twain's work and proud that she had heard him lecture. I don't think I ever saw her read a modem novel, but she knew all of Shakespeare, Dickens, Kipling and Longfellow and often quoted from their works. She subscribed to many magazines, not just Sunset and Ladies' Home Journal, but Atlantic, Harper's, New Republic, and The Nation. She also received the Daily Worker and some other far left newspaper, which together with her fervid letter writing and faithful contributions to suspect liberal causes, were probably what led to her being investigated by the FBI sometime in the 30's. She voted for Norman Thomas every time he ran. She saw nothing incongruous about her ownership of stock in United Fruit, General Foods and other corporate monsters.

She belonged to Women's International League for Peace and Freedom, the Sierra Club (she was a brisk walker), the Audubon Society, Cornell Women's Club and was very active in the politically liberal Unitarian Church, though at heart she remained a Quaker. (She believed Richard Nixon had no right to claim membership in the Society of Friends.) She was an easy mark for any charity that claimed to be feeding or helping poor people, children or minorities or conserving nature. She didn't give large amounts, probably $10 to $25, but she gave regularly and to ever increasing numbers of worthy causes. She had very definite opinions on social and political problems and would defend them fluently and heatedly.

She loved music and had an eclectic taste: Sousa marches, Strauss waltzes, Gilbert and Sullivan (snatches of which she would sing while doing housework), opera from Mozart through Wagner and on to Gershwin's Porgy and Bess. She took me to see both Porgy and Tristan and Isolde in the San Francisco opera house when I was in my teens. She didn't play any instrument or have much of a voice but she could carry a tune and often hummed or whistled as she went about the house. I enjoyed that and find myself humming some of the same melodies today.

When Gargo had a few minutes to spare, she would play a game of solitaire. She knew many different kinds and taught them to me, as well as other card games like Flinch and Russian Bank. She often read to me, at bedtime or when I was sick and she told wonderful stories about her girlhood and family.

She had another talent, which was for pithy (though often trite) expressions that I find myself uttering more often as I get older. Since she had lived at times in Germany and Switzerland these expressions were often sprinkled with a short phrase in one of the languages of those countries. Thus, surprise was expressed by "Heavens to Betsey," "Jumpin' Jehosaphat," or "Ach, du Lieber!" "Ye Gods and Little Fishes" was usually reserved for something really startling. Admonishment was, "Eat! Remember the starving children of Armenia," "Don't slump you're getting round shouldered," and "Mach' schnell!" Her humorous appraisal of individual behavior quirks was usually: "Between thee and me and the gatepost, everyone's a little crazy except thee and me and sometimes I wonder about thee." (She rarely used the Friends' pronoun except when speaking to other Quakers.) More serious disapproval or dismay elicited, "The world's going to the ding-dong bow-wows." This could be applied to anything from local scandals to worldwide political upheavals or social ills.

She rarely spoke a swear word but when pushed to extremity by hitting her thumb with a hammer or damaging something she treasured, she might let slip a Hell or a Damn. She also had a German phrase to help relieve frustration, something like, "Verflugtige Heilige Bimbam Himmel Donnerwetter Verdammt!"

Her favorite old maxims, besides the Golden Rule, were "Moderation in all things" or "Strike a happy medium" (which was also a family joke about hitting a cheerful clairvoyant.) Then there was "Waste not, want not," "Early to bed, early to rise' and "Make do with what you have."

She lived up to her own advice and was able to instill most of it in me, except the one about "Early to bed." She died in 1962 at the age of ninety-two, but her influence on my life is still very much a part of me. Though I rejected her tantrums and her Victorian strictness and prudishness, I absorbed much of her practical, down-to-earth approach to life, her independent spirit, her concern for the environment and for people less fortunate than we, her love of books, music, nature and travel and her ability to cope in difficult situations. I am thankful, now that she made me wear sensible shoes and stand up straight and eat my carrots. But I wish I could stop muttering, "The world is going to the ding dong bow wows!"

Important People
Helena

My sister, Helena, was my bane and my mentor. She was six years older than I and could do everything I wanted to do but couldn't. She could draw, play the piano and the violin, speak French and German, dance, walk on her hands, organize productions in which she and her girlfriends played dramatic roles like *Bluebeard and his Wives* while I was allowed to be a page, and perform for guests with enthusiasm and aplomb.

She was small and graceful with naturally curly blond hair (mine was straight and brown) and golden skin that tanned beautifully (mine burned and peeled). She not only excelled in school, she had numerous friends of both sexes. When I got to high school, six years after she had been there, the teachers and counselors would say, "Oh, are you Helena's sister? I didn't know she had a sister. What a talented girl!"

Of course, I owe my sister a lot, too. She taught me how to make linoleum block prints, how to talk on the telephone, how to dress and how to act with boys. She was my ally and fellow conspirator in fooling my mother and grandmother as to where we were going, who we were going with and what we would be doing while gone. We sometimes did the dishes together and once, with guilty giggles, we smuggled into the garbage can a dish brush we deemed too old and disgusting to use. Together we made fun of the temper tantrums, strict pronouncements, ridiculous airs and habits and terrible cooking of our guardians. She showed me how to put on lipstick on the way to the streetcar so our grandmother would not suspect our sinfulness.

Helena didn't always live at home with me. The years when I was three or four and again when I was seven to nine, she spent going to school in Switzerland and Germany, under the care of our grandmother. This difference in schooling served to widen the differences between us and deepen my feeling of being untalented, not good enough to warrant anything more than a public school education. For her part, my sister probably felt she was being banished from her family and friends, imprisoned with our Victorian grandmother, whose nickname was "Gargo" but whom we sometimes called "Gargoyle."

By the time Helena returned from her second stay abroad, she was almost sixteen and in her last semester of high school — a stranger to my ten-year-old self. Within weeks, her dirndl dress, loden cloth cape and hair in a bun were gone, replaced by sweaters, skirts, saddle shoes and a curly blond bob.

As the Great Depression hung on, my family was forced to rent rooms to increase our income, and so my sister and I shared a bedroom for the first time. By the time I was twelve and she was eighteen, I had become very aware of Helena's numerous boyfriends. There were gatherings of young musicians at our house, Sunday waffle suppers when the family got to inspect a series of polite but nervous young men, and many, many phone calls.

My voice sounded much like my sister's on the phone and I used to amuse myself by briefly pretending to be her and getting to hear endearments meant for her from her current swain. Once I answered a piano serenade from the young man who lived in the apartment across the walk. He and my sister had been playing Beethoven's Moonlight Sonata to each other, but when I got to the difficult second movement I had to give

OVERCOMING CHILDHOOD ADVANTAGES

Off to Europe aboard the Berengaria, 1926.

Donkey ride in Sicily.

Older sister, Helena, age nine-and-a-half, instructs little sister, Rosalie, age three-and-a-half, atop Notre Dame de Paris.

up my pretense and be exposed as an imposter. Helena's senior year in college, when I was 13 and she was 19, she had a serious love affair. My parents did not approve of this suitor and so some secrecy was necessary. She would come home late to our bedroom, from supposedly studying in the library, and, though I pretended to be half asleep, I could tell she looked disheveled and she had a strange odor. She always got out of her clothes quickly and headed for the bathroom before my mother could come upstairs and check that she was in for the night. It was all very fascinating!

My sister's birth mother had died in the influenza epidemic when Helena was only two years old. When my parents married she was four and had been living with relatives on a ranch near Sebastopol where, according to my mother and grandmother, she had been allowed to "run wild." She was not always truthful or well mannered and sometimes forgot to go to the bathroom in the house. She must have been a real trial to these two proper Quaker ladies as they struggled to civilize her according to Berkeley standards. When I was born, two years after the marriage, my mother was delighted; now she and my grandmother had an unformed lump of clay to mold into the perfect child. My mother could prove that her daughter was more brilliant, beautiful and admirable than the child of my father's first wife (whose name was never mentioned in our household).

Helena's mother had been an artist and Helena had already displayed talent in art and music, so though I was encouraged to draw and given piano lessons for ten years, no one really expected me to outshine my six years older sister. Instead I was programmed to be the "scientific" one, like my botanist mother. I was supposed to aim for a graduate degree in science, or better yet, an M.D. This comparison and competition went on all the years my sister and I were growing up, each of us feeling that the other was the favored one — The Best Daughter. The atmosphere did not foster a close relationship between us. Helena escaped into graduate school when I was fourteen, then into marriage, and I, too, left home to marry immediately after college graduation. It was our way of rebelling: We would stay home and be good wives and mothers instead of pursuing careers as we were expected to do. (Of course, it wasn't many years before we got bored with that and went to work anyway.)

After we had children of our own, my sister and I compared notes, baby-sat for each other, fostered our children's friendships with their cousins and commiserated over our mother's meddling in our child-rearing methods. The difference in our ages, which had seemed vast before, became as nothing when I was twenty-four and she was thirty. Still, we did not become close. We lived in different parts of the state and our worlds were utterly dissimilar. She still belonged to the Berkeley university world of Art, Music and Ideas, and I had become a suburban Sacramento housewife with little opportunity to enjoy cultural events or intellectual stimulation. When I visited Berkeley, I would get the same line I got in high school: "You're Helena's sister? I didn't know she had a sister!"

I finally returned to Berkeley from Aptos in the fall of 2002. My husband had died in 1989, and I was feeling the need of some help from my children and grandchildren, several of whom lived in Berkeley. Helena was 85 by then, but still petite with curly, shoulder length hair (more ash than blond) and fashionable clothes that to me seemed more suitable for someone 50 years younger. She wore bright colors, large dangly earrings, and until hip surgery grounded her, very high heels. Her four sons affectionately called her "Flashy." She had a regular beau, a retired professor in his nineties, who squired her to concerts, lectures, art openings and faculty parties, but their relationship was platonic.

She and I enjoyed many family gatherings and cultural affairs together but she died very suddenly of heart failure the day after Thanksgiving, 2004. I miss her a lot and wish I could ask her all the questions I still have about family and local history.

Important People
WTS

I began to know my father when he was eighty-eight. He needed my help in arranging care for my seventy-eight year old mother who had slid into senile dementia and could no longer be cared for by him alone. And so I took a leave from my job in a city 100 miles away and moved back into my childhood home that I had left when I was twenty.

Walter Theodore Steilberg, or WTS, as he always signed himself, was not a substantial presence in the matriarchal household of my childhood. He, too, had been raised by women — a maiden aunt and fifteen-year-older sister in addition to his mother — to be a proper Victorian gentleman. I saw him at mealtimes, when he was often late or had to leave hurriedly for some appointment or deadline. His work as an architect and engineer was the passion of his life and guided all his actions. He usually ate rapidly and then pulled out his slide rule to do some urgent calculations while waiting for dessert. If he didn't have his slide rule, a napkin and pencil would do. Or he would excuse himself from the table and retreat to his top floor study.

He was invariably kind to me in an absentminded way — smiled, patted my shoulder and asked me about school — but I never felt as if he really listened to what I had to say. Still, I felt less stressed with him than with my mother or grandmother because he never created a scene, rarely lost his temper or raised his voice, and handled conflict by retiring from it. Occasionally, one of the women would attack him verbally in a way even

OVERCOMING CHILDHOOD ADVANTAGES

he could not tolerate, and then he would defend himself with his version of the truth, ending with, "Put that in your pipe and smoke it!" before stalking out of the room. His anger was more often directed at incompetent workmen, crooked politicians or greedy capitalists than at his own family.

Since my mother worked, my grandmother was the cook for our family and her cuisine was largely bland, unimaginative and overdone. My father usually ate it without complaint but he was fussy about certain things and my grandmother accommodated him in these. He would not eat onions, tomato sauce, or any milk product that was white, though he loved orange cheese and chocolate ice cream. His fried eggs had to be hard all the way through with burnt lace edges; nothing could be runny or soft and any meat had to be cooked to a leathery dark brown. He much preferred fish and touted it as "brain food." He loved fresh fruit and ate oranges every day but never a salad or other raw vegetables. And he drank strong, black coffee all day long, sometimes adding a dollop of whiskey in the evenings. He liked to brag that coffee did not keep him awake, but as with his Scandinavian ancestors, it helped to do so.

In those pre-World War II days, he always wore a dark suit, white shirt and tie, over a one piece union suit and socks with garters. When he left the house, he added a topcoat and fedora. Only his closest friend called him Walter (never Walt); to all others he was "Mr. Steilberg."

When he wasn't working in his office at home he was just rushing out the door to catch the train and ferry to San Francisco or to meet someone who would give him a ride to a construction site. He never drove a car but was a prodigious walker — to the blueprint shop in downtown Berkeley or to the campus for some meeting or consultation. These departures from home were always stressful times because he could never find his glasses (he had three pairs of trifocals, always dirty) or his briefcase or his hat and whoever was at home had to make a desperate last minute search for the missing object. His returns home in the evening were much calmer, pleasanter events unless my mother was waiting to pick a fight with him. Often he would whistle as he came up the long brick walk to our house, two of his favorites being Gluck's "Dance of the Blessed Spirits" and Bach's "Air for G String." Another sound that heralded his approach was throat clearing, a sort of elephantine trumpeting which my mother said was due to allergies and my grandmother said was just a nervous habit.

My father didn't work all the time. On Sunday afternoons, at my mother's sometimes shrill insistence, he would take walks with us in the Berkeley hills. He would go to a concert at the University or to dinner at the Black Sheep and a local movie with my mother. And when, occasionally, he would have friends over for tea or dinner he would become his warm, sociable self, knowledgeable about history, geography, politics, as well as art and architecture, and a great storyteller. But I had no part in these conversations.

Sometimes my father was gone from home completely. During my early childhood he often would spend a week or so at Hearst's rising San Simeon Castle where he was structural consultant and designer for Julia Morgan. When I was eight, he went to Spain for several months in order to supervise the disassembling, crating and shipping of an entire monastery Hearst had purchased. He was greatly admired by the contractors, students and other architects he worked with for his utter integrity and honesty. He was very modest and never flaunted or even took credit for many of his accomplishments (it was my mother who did that), but the other side of that trait was that he detested bragging and self aggrandizement in others: he regarded Frank Lloyd Wright as something of a charlatan and even Bernard Maybeck he found to be a little too fond of

OVERCOMING CHILDHOOD ADVANTAGES

publicity. And yet he worked for many years for Hearst and considered him to be a fascinating, and in many ways, an admirable man in spite of his flamboyance, his ruthless wielding of power and his often questionable taste in art.

Berkeley was home to a number of uncloseted homosexual couples, even in the twenties and thirties, and though some of these were my father's professional associates and belonged to my parents' social circle, my father was never comfortable with the idea of any kind of unconventional sex. He handled his discomfort by poking fun in a gentle way, referring to Berkeley's "fruits and nuts" and executing his most distinctive gesture of scorn: he would hold his nose and with his other hand brush the hair on top of his head forward over his forehead. This gesture was also used for corny music, gushy people or sentimental pronouncements.

There were two brief periods during these first twenty years of my life when I got to be the focus of my father's attention and to be alone with him. The first was when I was thirteen and struggling with geometry. My mother enlisted him to tutor me and several nights a week after supper, the rest of the family would vacate the living room and Father and I would have a session with my homework. Mostly I remember these times as periods of great frustration for my father and feelings of unworthiness for myself. We both tried very hard and were uncomfortable every minute of the time, though I did get enough insight to raise my grade from a C to a B.

The other time we spent time together was when I worked for him a few weeks one summer when I was about seventeen. He had a small office in San Francisco then, close to the train terminal at Third and Townsend, and I was supposed to help him sort and file his papers and drawings. I enjoyed dressing up to go to the City every morning, riding the train across the bridge with my father and going to lunch with him usually at Manning's. I'm sure it was my mother's idea to introduce me to the world of work in this least demanding way, and I sometimes had the feeling that my father didn't know quite what he wanted me to do to help him. But I had him to myself and when he wasn't busy he actually talked to me as another adult about San Francisco, about the places he had been, jobs he had worked on, people he worked for and with, some of them famous like W.R. Hearst and Julia Morgan. I was thrilled at all this attention and fell a little in love with him but then I went back to college and he went on to more engrossing work and we resumed our old patterns of polite non communication.

Then, in April 1942, at the age of 56, WTS went off to Kodiak, Alaska, where he spent the next four years as structural engineer for the U.S. Navy Base there. When he returned I was married and living away from Berkeley and our visits and conversations over the next thirty years were brief and mostly centered on grandchildren. His Alaska experience had changed many of my father's habits. He no longer wore suits or other formal dress but favored Loden cloth jackets and pants in olive drab, such as rangers wear, with casual desert boots and berets. He grew a beautiful white beard and after a serious knee infection he walked with a cane, though still briskly. He had lived alone in a small cabin on Kodiak and had learned to cook simple meals for himself and to wash his dishes and clothes, though I never saw him darn a sock, iron a shirt or use a dust mop. He brought back from Kodiak a black Labrador retriever, Chum, and a large, fluffy grey tomcat, Timmy, who had been his companions there and he doted on those pets, as he did all his animals. One of his delights was training a blue jay to take peanuts from his hand. He named the jay "Goober."

Then my mother's illness brought me back to my childhood

home and to living with my father every day. The task facing us was enormous: Clear a large three story house of the accumulated possessions of more than fifty years so that it could be rented, the income needed to pay my mother's huge nursing home bills. Then prepare a small cottage on the same property as a place where, eventually, my mother could be brought and cared for in familiar surroundings under my father's loving supervision. In addition, my father was trying to organize his professional papers, drawings and books to give to the University and was being interviewed by the Bancroft Library oral history people.

He was eighty-eight years old, distraught about his finances, brokenhearted over my mother's hopeless illness, exhausted and confused by all the decisions required of him.

My husband and I spent four months living with him and doing everything we could to help him. He never broke down but many times I would find him sitting with his head in his hands, his face in its longest Scandinavian expression of gloom, his hair rumpled. Through many shared meals, trips to the nursing home, errands, shopping excursions and problem-solving sessions, we grew closer than we had ever been in my childhood and he would often pat me or hug me and tell me how much he appreciated me. Once he even told me that he wished he had spent more time in his life with his wife and daughters and less time on his work.

Often there were people from the University or professional friends at the house and then my father would emerge from his gloom and become the charming raconteur again. And he entertained my husband and me at dinner with wonderful tales of his life in Berkeley and San Francisco, San Simeon, Rome, Spain, Kodiak, Saudi Arabia, Hawaii and other places he had worked. When I finally felt I was really getting to know him, a car hit him one dark, rainy night on his way to the nursing home to take treats to my mother. He lived four days, his mind still alert in his broken body, and the last words he said to me were, "If they'd just bring me a cheese and pumpernickel sandwich and a decent cup of coffee I could be out of here!"

Important People
Granny Plans

My mother, Elizabeth, was wonderful at making plans. She always knew what other people should do and the best way for them to go about doing it. Her first career was as a botanist, but when the Great Depression forced her to find a paying job, she switched to social work and found her niche for life. My grandmother liked to tell a story about Elizabeth, her only child. On her first day at kindergarten, the four year old girl noticed that one of the little boys remained sitting in his chair instead of marching around the room to music, as the rest of the class was doing. Elizabeth grabbed this miscreant by his shirt, pulled him to his feet and marched him around the room in front of her. She knew what was right for other people, even then.

Elizabeth's father disappeared from her life when she was only two years old, first through hospitalization, and two years later by death. So she and her mother, Mary Effie, had an extremely close and frequently abrasive relationship. They returned to live with Mary Effie's parents and Grandfather Van Everen became Elizabeth's surrogate father. But he, too, died suddenly, when she was twelve, leaving her in a world of women again. These were educated, strong-willed Quaker women, and much was expected of Elizabeth. She was a beautiful girl who excelled in her studies and dreamed of becoming a doctor. At UC Berkeley, where she graduated in 1918, she was elected to Phi Beta Kappa and Sigma Xi, the male-dominated science honor society. She had at least two serious suitors but turned them down and went on to get her Master's in Botany. I don't know why she didn't go to medical school. She claimed her health was not strong enough, but she had tremendous vitality and I believe she was afraid to break away from her mother and grandmother, with whom she had formed a tight little threesome since her grandfather died. She went to work as a research assistant for Willis Lynn Jepson, her botany professor (who was also in love with her) and continued to live at home.

When my grandmother, Mary Effie, decided it was time to build a home for the three women in the Berkeley hills, she hired a young architect who lived in the neighborhood. While the house was being built, the architect and my mother fell in love and were married in 1921. When the house was completed, he moved in with the three women. My father brought to the marriage his daughter by his first wife, Rowena, who had died in the flu epidemic of 1919. This little girl, my half sister Helena, was now four years old and since her mother's death had been living on a ranch near Sebastopol. My mother and grandmother believed she had been allowed to "run wild" there; she had occasional "accidents" and was not always truthful. They had a real challenge on their hands in civilizing this child. When I was born, two years later, my mother's interest in botany was replaced by her overwhelming interest in child development — mine. She read every modern book on the subject, attended classes at the University Child Guidance Institute and recorded every move and sound I made. The record keeping, I believe, was partly scientific curiosity, partly an expression of love and pride and partly an opportunity to prove to all concerned that her baby was superior to her predecessor's child.

The good things I remember about my mother are her beauty and her kindness. She had lovely classic features and waist length dark hair that she braided and wound around her head in a crown, a process I never tired of watching. When I was very small she would sometimes sing me a bedtime song Brahms' "Lullaby" or "Speed, Bonnie Boat" and I loved her clear, light voice. She was always doing things for friends and neighbors as well as family — offering advice, a meal, a place to stay or a ride. She was the only person in our family who could drive a car, and in spite of working full time, she hauled me to ice skating and dancing lessons, youth group meetings, Camp Fire camp and more. She would use her precious weekends and vacations to take me on excursions (my father almost always stayed home to work). We went to Carmel, to Yosemite by way of the old Tioga Road from the east, to the Pasadena Rose Parade, to Tahoe and Fallen Leaf Lake and to our friends' ranch in Sonoma County.

She stood up for me with my grandmother, who had the day-to-day job of raising me, but whom my mother considered too Victorian in her approach. I soon learned to play these two to my advantage: "Mother said I could..." or "Gargo said I could..." Of course, there were loud arguments about what was best for me but my mother almost always prevailed. So if I appealed to my mother's ideas of modern child rearing, I might get to stay up a little later, wear my skirts at a more fashionable length or have some dessert without eating every bite of my dinner.

The bad things which made my mother hard to live with were her great need for me to be The Best and to have that excellence recognized by everyone; her need to run everyone's life according to her idea of what was best for them; and her lifelong frustration and anger at not always being able to control the actions of others. She longed for my father to pay as much attention to her as he did to his work. She resented my grandmother's running of the house even as she depended on her help. She despaired of my ever outshining my talented older sister. And her anger was expressed in noisy, dramatic ways, terrifying to a child. Her tantrums were behavior she learned from my grandmother and many a suppertime was ruined by one or the other of them yelling and banging out of the dining room, stomping up the stairs and giving a final slam to her bedroom door that would shake the whole house. These scenes could be triggered by a careless remark that the peas were a little overdone or that the newspaper was missing.

My mother's tantrums outdid Gargo's, though. When she was really angry, usually at something my father did or didn't do, she would roll on the floor, kicking and screaming like a two year old. Worst of all were the times she would grab her car keys and run out the door, yelling that she was going to crash and kill herself. For years, I half believed her, in spite of reassurances from my father and grandmother.

Though my mother exerted tremendous pressure in our family, she was never able to completely control my father or grandmother. My father simply disappeared into his work and my grandmother did a lot of traveling. When my mother went to work full time, in 1930, she abdicated the running of the household and my grandmother took over. Gargo was the one who was there when I came home from school, who went to the doctor appointments, school conferences and shoe shopping with me, who helped me with my homework, who played games with me in the evening and who nursed me when I was sick. In that sense, my mother ceded control over my life to her mother, but I was never in doubt about who was the final authority. My mother made the decisions about with whom I could play, where I could go, how late I could stay up, what school I should go to and what sort of lessons I should take. Later, it was what University I should attend, what subject I should major in, what sorority I should join and what sort of boy I should date.

After I had children of my own, I was given endless counsel on how to raise them. My mother was very helpful about baby-sitting, taking time off from her work and even using her vacation time to be able to supervise her grandchildren. I believe she thought her interest and participation in their care and development gave her the right to tell me how to raise them. She took them on trips, bought them nice clothes and expensive toys and paid for special lessons. It was a controlling sort of love that maddened me even as I accepted its benefits. When my grandchildren began to arrive, my mother was still using the same tactics.

The term "Granny Plans" was invented by my children in their early adulthood as a way of describing, humorously, my mother's obsession with making, often very complicated, sometimes very sensible plans for arranging the lives of those around her. For any move, change, visit, expedition or proposal involving family, we would be presented with these plans for accomplishing whatever was proposed in the best possible way. The solutions could be so involved and convoluted we would forget the problem they were supposed to solve. However, a rejection of the plans could be met with hostility or unsettling psychiatric interpretations from my mother. Now, when my middle-aged children want to needle me about making arrangements that seem to me to be both sensible and creative, they tell me I am making "Granny Plans."

Dr. Kübler Ross, Meet Dr. Kevorkian

The phone calls from my father had been getting increasingly frantic and frequent. He was eighty-eight years old and trying to care for my seventy-eight year old mother whose mental disintegration was becoming unbearable to him. She still had tremendous physical vitality, and though he was a healthy, active old man, he could not control her. She prowled the house at night, fearful of imaginary "bands of black men" and other evildoers who were out to get her. My father lost so much sleep trying to calm and reassure her that he found his daytime responsibilities of shopping, cooking, washing her clothes, paying the bills and keeping her from harming herself or him to be exhausting. She drove away any help he tried to hire, once with a butcher knife. There was also the emotional exhaustion of watching his brilliant, beautiful wife sliding into madness.

I lived in Sacramento, 85 miles form Berkeley, and had a stressful, full-time job so I was not much help to him. But this latest, desperate phone call, in June of 1974, was to let me know that my mother was in the Psych Ward at Herrick Hospital on 72-hour observation. She had had another one of her tantrums over something my father did or did not do for her and had run out into the street and lain down in the middle of narrow, curving Panoramic Way in order to "end it all." My father could not move her and had called the authorities for help, an action for which he was now berating himself.

OVERCOMING CHILDHOOD ADVANTAGES

Of course, my husband and I took off from work and headed for Berkeley immediately. I found my mother on the top floor of the hospital in a locked ward. She had been neatly dressed in one of the tasteful outfits my father had probably helped her choose, but her long hair, usually braided and coiled into a crown, had been too much for the aides and had simply been brushed out and skinned tightly back from her face into a long pony tail. She looked old and pale and was so stoned on tranquilizers that any reasonable conversation was impossible. But she did seem to understand that she would have to go to some other place for care before she could go back home. My father had finally admitted that he could not care for her by himself.

My sister and I spent the next two days visiting a series of those dismal storage places known as Convalescent Hospitals. We had already investigated and ruled out a number of them. Now there was the additional problem that my mother was physically strong but emotionally very difficult to manage; many places were not equipped to handle someone from the Psych Ward. Finally, my father found a small, homey "guest house" within easy walking distance of his home. (He did not drive a car.) My mother was transferred there by ambulance when the 72-hour hold was over, and we did everything we could think of to make her feel at home there: favorite night clothes, snacks, magazines, radio, afghan and pillows. But early the next morning my father was notified that he must find another place for her; she had "escaped" and was found wandering along College Avenue.

I don't know why my father picked a nursing home miles away, in Castro Valley. My sister and I took him to see several that day, and that one must have seemed more humane or less expensive to him. But it meant that after I returned to Sacramento he had to hire someone to drive him out there several times a week. He always took my mother special treats an avocado or peach, Triscuits and cheese, chocolates or toffee candy. Visiting her there was very painful for him and for me.

After she tried to escape again by climbing over the garden wall, the nurses kept her so doped up that she spoke very little. She would sit in her chair, smiling and nodding, while I chattered inanely and a pool of urine formed beneath her chair. My sister refused to visit.

In the fall, I took a leave of absence from my job while my husband (who had retired early) and I lived with my father and worked on clearing out the big family home, crammed with 50 years worth of possessions and junk. We needed to rent the place to pay the nursing home fees. My father was in serious financial trouble because of my mother's medical bills. Also, he was trying to get his books, architectural drawings and personal papers in order for the University and was preparing a place to bring my mother home so she could be cared for there. Then, in November, my mother got pneumonia. She was in intensive care, and I believe would have died then if my father had been able to let her go. The hospital social worker requested interviews with both my sister and me separately. With both of us, the discussion centered around: "Why is your father so determined to keep your mother alive?" though this was not stated in so many words. My sister and I both felt that our father was distraught and tormented with guilt for all the years he had neglected my mother for his work, and he felt he must make it up to her now.

My mother did not die then, but she was bedridden from that time on unable to feed herself or care for her personal needs in any way, rarely speaking except to voice her pain and unhappiness, rarely recognizing anyone except my father. She was moved to another nursing home closer to Berkeley, where my father could go by bus to visit her. He went every day, sometimes twice a day, taking the treats he liked to feed her.

OVERCOMING CHILDHOOD ADVANTAGES

He was heartbroken at her condition, frustrated at the minimal care she was receiving and desperate over his finances. My husband and I continued to clean out the family home, working six hours a day every day for four months, so that the bulk of the large house would be ready for tenants. My father designed and built a concrete wheelchair ramp from the street level up to the small cottage on the property where he hoped to house my mother with someone to care for her.

Early in December my husband and I returned to Sacramento for a few days to take care of our affairs there. One evening the phone rang, and it was one of my sister's sons, choking on his sobs, telling us that my father had been hit by a car and was in the hospital in critical condition. An older driver, also in his late eighties, struck him on a dark and rainy evening. My father was hit on the way to the bus to make his second trip of the day to the nursing home to take goodies to my mother. He was hit as he crossed Piedmont Avenue in front of International House, a crossing he had made thousands of times in his life.

My husband and I left for Berkeley at once and found my father with a fractured skull and a crushed pelvis, hooked up to every machine, catheter and IV bottle in the ICU, but still feisty and worrying about my mother not getting her treats. By the next day he was making plans for his recuperation ("Good I got that wheelchair ramp done."), still with the goal of being able to bring my mother home when he was recovered. He groused about the "damn tubes" when what he wanted was a cheese sandwich and a cup of coffee. It took him four days to die, during which time the doctors tried some risky, possibly lifesaving surgery, but in the end his 88-year-old heart just stopped, worn out and defeated. By the time we made it to the hospital after the nurse phoned, he was gone.

I didn't know how to tell my mother what had happened; it seemed too difficult for me to do just then. My mother didn't seem to understand anything you told her anyway. She often thought I was her mother. But my older daughter had more courage than I. She insisted that her grandmother must be told of my father's death and that she, Joanna, would tell her. I did not go with her to deliver the message, but Joanna reported back that my mother showed no reaction at all to the news and for the next three years, until her own death, she continued to call for "Walter" to do things for her.

My mother did get to come back to her home in Berkeley for those last years of her life. She was cared for by Joanna and a series of women who came in to help with bathing, changing, feeding, bed making and lifting her into her wheelchair so she could look outdoors. The wheelchair ramp proved to be useless because it was not possible to push her on the steep, bumpy side hill paths around the property. She never got any clearer mentally and her arthritis was so painful that she screamed when she was touched. She was such a pitiful sight that none of her former friends could bear to visit her. Many times she asked for someone to help her "end it all." She had a couple of bouts with pneumonia and finally succumbed to that "old person's friend" because Joanna was strong enough to allow that to happen without sending her back to the hospital to have her life prolonged another time. Many times during those years I wished there had been someone like Dr. Kevorkian around.

HOME ENTERTAINMENT

I spent a lot of time alone as a child. My sister, being six years older, was not a very satisfactory playmate, and besides, she was at school in Europe when I was three and four and again when I was seven to nine. There were only a few children my age in the neighborhood and when they weren't available I had to find ways of amusing myself.

I could read before I went to school and I spent many hours with the Beatrix Potter books and A.A. Milne. I had stuffed versions of Winnie the Pooh, Tigger, Eeyore and Kanga so I could act out the stories or make up my own. But I also enjoyed Milne's book of rhymes, *Now We Are Six*. Then came Kipling's *Jungle Books*, *The Wizard of Oz*, *The Secret Garden* and *The Little Princess* and a whole series of books about twins from different lands who always dressed in folk costumes. Under one of the window seats in the living room, we had a set of bound Saint Nicholas magazines from my mother's childhood that I was allowed to look at on rainy days. I especially loved fairy tales from many countries, my favorite being *East of the Sun and West of the Moon* which was stories from Scandinavia. I knew all the Greek and Roman myths by heart. Of course, I was read to also, which got me off to a good start. As I grew older, I read *Treasure Island* and Alcott's *Little Women* series, but by the time I finished with all the trials and triumphs of Jo, Beth, Meg and Amy, they seemed pretty smarmy to me. In addition to Milne's verses, the poetry of Eugene Fields and

Stevenson's *A Child's Garden of Verses* were my favorites and I tried to emulate them in my own attempts to write poems.

I had a set of stone blocks in dull blue, cream and rosy brick colors, in many shapes and sizes, from which I could construct elaborate castles and towns. I also collected, with my allowance, many glass marbles of all colors, patterns and sizes. Though I never got good at playing the game of marbles, I used them with my blocks to represent kings, queens, knights, princes, princesses and servants, a whole cast of inhabitants for my castles. These games gave me such a sense of power and control in my adult dominated world that I kept on playing them until I was nearly twelve and was ashamed to be caught doing something so childish. I had the same problem giving up my large family of dolls from many lands.

My pets were very important to me also, especially the big, black German Shepherd named Nero we got as a puppy when I was seven. He was a friendly, loving dog, protective of children, gentle and tolerant of kittens and smaller dogs that wanted to play with him. He was my guardian and fun-loving companion in all my outdoor activities and was thrilled to go for walks with me. All our pets had to have distinctive names. The cats were Galahad or Guinevere or Brunhilde but Felicia Fluff was the only one who would allow me to dress her in doll clothes and wheel her in a buggy. The cat we had the longest was Dunkel, a big, white neutered tom who always looked rather dingy except right after one of his infrequent and stressful baths. Hence his name, which means "dark" in German and was supposed to be a joke, but my friends had to have it explained to them.

We also had rabbits for a while, then ducks both having arrived as Easter-present babies. I liked to gather greens for the rabbits; milkweed was their favorite but when I lost interest in them (they didn't do much) they were given to our household helper, Mrs. Callavaro, for a nice rabbit stew. I felt bad about that. The ducks were kept for a while, supposedly to reduce the snail population in the garden, but they proved to be eating more plants than snails and they left nasty grey green globs all over the terraces. Going barefoot was really risky and I wasn't sorry to see them go.

Outdoors, my favorite activities were tree climbing, hopscotch, jump rope, the swing and rings, roller skating and riding my bicycle. Just down the hill a little was a big flat area in front of the UC football stadium. It is now a parking lot, but then it was a turnaround for the end of Prospect Street, with a central circle of grass and a prickly evergreen tree in the middle. The nearby houses were all sororities or fraternities. It was a great place to skate or learn to ride a bike. On the slope down to this area were a lot of thick bushes with red berries where I used to hide my bike while I played in the stadium. The gate at one end of the stadium was left open until 4:30 on some days, but if it wasn't I knew where I could go under or over the fence to get in. It was great fun to play ball or just run around the field and up and down the tiers of seats. The neighborhood kids and I played hide-and-seek in the labyrinthine passages under the bleachers. One day I left my bike and when I came back it was gone! It wasn't a fancy bike; this was the Depression and my mother had gotten it for $18 at the Salvation Army, but I was outraged and crushed.

My sister was good at dancing, tumbling and gymnastics and I wanted to be likewise. With her help, I learned to do somersaults, cartwheels, a handstand, walk on my hands (briefly) and some Isadora Duncan style dance movements. I was about six then and my sister was twelve. What I really wanted to be able to do was to fly. I practiced often, leaping off the five foot high terraces, the pergola, the playhouse roof and out of trees flapping my arms wildly. After many months of this I became convinced I could fly for about thirty seconds not off a wall but by jumping straight up in the air and hovering there. I never seemed able to increase my time aloft and I finally gave up, though I still dreamed of flying.

My preschool friends had moved or drifted away and I had no one my age to play with so I started playing with a few littler children who lived nearby. All of them were at least four years younger than I and they would do anything I told them to do! I held school for them in the playhouse, with slates, chalk, paper and crayons and may actually have taught them something; at least, their mothers were very grateful to me for taking care of them and gave me cookies when I came around. My mother and grandmother needled me by calling them "Rosalie's kindergarten." They wanted me to bring home friends from school but my classmates seemed to live too far away or to have other things to do. My mother was the only one in the family who could drive a car and she was at work.

In the evenings after supper, my grandmother would always play a game with me before bedtime. Sometimes my sister or mother joined in, but my father always went back to work in his study. (I don't think I ever saw him play a game, though he loved to listen to football games at Cal.) The rest of us played several kinds of double solitaire, Russian Bank, Hearts, Rummy, Flinch, and a series of card games that came from Europe. The cards were Highly Educational; they had pictures of famous art, artists, musicians or writers of different periods, along with descriptions in German, French and Italian. Four Italian Renaissance musicians, or Dutch painters or 18th century German poets made a "book" and the one with the most "books" won. We also played board games, my favorites being Parcheesi, Chinese Checkers and Pirate and Traveler.

My family did other nice things together. Every afternoon at 4:00 we had tea and my father, if he was home, stopped work and came downstairs when I rang the little brass bell.

OVERCOMING CHILDHOOD ADVANTAGES

My mother worked away from home, starting when I was seven, so she was there only on weekends. Sometimes neighbors would drop in to chat. I was allowed to have Cambric Tea, which was hot water and milk with maybe a teaspoon of real tea for color. Often, at teatime, the talk would be travel tales of Europe or the Orient. My parents and Gargo, especially, had traveled many places and had many experiences to recall and relate. Since I could remember almost nothing about the one time I went to Europe, at age three-and-a-half, I felt pretty left out. But sometimes the talk would be about me and what cute thing I had said or done in Lausanne or Carcasonne or Pompeii and then I would squirm with embarrassment and wish I could disappear.

Another family ritual was walking in the hills above our home on sunny Sunday afternoons. My mother insisted on this time of togetherness; we would all be ready to go, with Nero jumping around and barking in excitement, and my father would still be up in his study, working. It would take my mother several shrill whistles on the speaking tube and usually an ear piercing shriek to get him to come down. By then, my sister and I often wished we had gone without him, but once we got going I enjoyed myself. We climbed to the top of Panoramic Hill past all the homes, and on up one of the fire trails, across the grassy slopes, with all of San Francisco Bay in view, to the top of Strawberry Canyon. Here there were many bay trees and one huge one we called The Big Bay, whose branches were made for climbing on or sitting for a snack or picnic. The spicy fragrance of the leaves was wonderful. Sometimes I went there with only Nero for company. He would dash ahead of me and then return, stopping only to dig furiously at gopher holes. As far as I know, he never caught a gopher but his persistent and exuberant pursuit, even in the face of repeated frustration, may have been a lesson to me.

CHRISTMAS TIME

The family times I enjoyed most were our holiday celebrations and Christmas was the best. It started with putting up the tree which, before we had a car, was delivered by the grocer's boy. It was usually a modest five or six feet tall and was always put in the same place, on a window seat at the end of the living room near the piano. For many years it was placed in the same deep jade green Chinese jar which meant that the wooden stand and the lower branches of the tree had to be cut short enough to fit in the jar. The jar was then filled with small rocks to keep the tree standing firm and finally, water was added to keep the tree fresh. My father was supposed to do this job but he took so long getting around to it that my grandmother usually did it. In later years, we just stood the tree on the window seat or floor and swathed the base in cotton batting sprinkled with glitter.

Then we bought fresh cranberries and popped popcorn and sat around the dining room table threading long red and white chains to drape on the tree. My grandmother always made gingerbread men, angels, stars and bells (with much help from me in licking the pan) and the cookies were threaded as ornaments, too, along with little candy canes, both of which had to be hung out of reach of our German Shepherd, Nero. Even so, the gingerbread men usually disappeared before Christmas Day arrived. My mother and grandmother had a really beautiful, unusual collection of ornaments from countries where they had traveled — little carved, wooden animals from Germany or Switzerland, tiny dolls in bright costumes from France, Italy or Spain — as well as shiny strings of colored beads and bangles from my mother's childhood.

When I was very young, we used real candles on the tree, electric ones being scorned by my parents as parvenu. A pail of water was kept near the tree and the candles were never lit unless an adult was present. The small flames made a lovely, soft glow reflected in the shiny ornaments and in the window behind the tree. Later on we did have strings of many colored electric lights which had to go on the tree first instead of last, like the candles. They all had to be tested ahead of time because they were wired in such a way that if one light on a string went out, all the others did, too.

My favorite tree trimming job was draping the tinsel icicles on the branches when the tree was all trimmed. I didn't just throw handfuls at the tree but placed each strand very carefully, a compulsion which may have led to my being deemed fit for a career in science. When I was tall enough and steady enough to climb up on a step stool, I was allowed to place the special silver star on the tip of the tree. For two weeks before and a week after Christmas the living room's rather somber look was brightened up and the place smelled like a pine forest.

Our Christmas cards were always homemade, though I expect my grandmother bought conventional ones for some of her old lady friends, usually to benefit a worthy organization. My parents' cards were often a picture taken by my father, who had an early Leica and was an excellent photographer. These pictures rarely looked Christmassy in the commercial sense. They could be scenic — a view of the sun setting in the Golden Gate or of fireworks on Carmel Beach — or they might be a beautiful design symbolizing Peace, or something gently humorous like a blue jay perched on my mother's finger or our big black police dog with a white kitten. They always featured something that was a part of our lives in some way. My mother was in charge of who they got sent to, many of them people I had never heard of, but my father usually had last minute additions to the long list when he remembered some business associate who should be included. My sister was a gifted artist and sketched or watercolored her cards which were the envy of six-years-younger me, who was still bumbling around with crayons and colored pencils. Finally, my sister got into mass production with linoleum block printing and taught me how to do it. I must have gouged my fingers and taken unplanned nicks out of my blocks many times but I found I could make a simple shape like a star, tree or angel (the cookie cutters helped) and, when printed with colored ink on different colored paper, it looked quite attractive. My attempt at a reindeer was frustrating, though, and it turned out with a big gap in one antler.

On Christmas Eve we all sang carols around the piano, with my sister at the keyboard. We did all the traditional ones but prided ourselves on singing some in their original language. I learned 0, *Tannenbaum, Stille Nacht, Heilige Nacht,* and *Adeste Fideles* before I knew the English words. My sister and grandmother had brought back some books of carols from Germany and France and we sang some of these, though I never could pronounce the French right.

Christmas Day began with opening our stockings which my sister and I usually borrowed from our grandmother because she had long, sturdy tan lisle ones that held a lot. There was always an orange in the toe and little things like jacks, marbles, a jump rope or colored pencils. The stockings were heavily thumb tacked to the mantel over the dining room fireplace. We left cookies and milk nearby for Santa and the next morning they were always gone, but after I was about eight and became a nonbeliever, I think the custom stopped.

OVERCOMING CHILDHOOD ADVANTAGES

Opening the presents under the tree had to wait until we were all dressed and breakfasted and we had to keep out of the living room until then but we did a lot of peeking through the glass doors from the hall and dining room. Usually my father, who always put off his shopping until Christmas Eve, was still fussing around trying to find wrapping paper or someone to wrap a present for him. When it was finally time for us to go into the living room there wasn't any scrambling for presents. I think the adults took turns being "Santa Claus" and handed out the gifts one at a time, in rotation, while everyone else watched. Sometimes it was hard to put on a big show of enthusiasm over a box of socks or underwear, not infrequent gifts during the Depression. But I got thrilling gifts, too—Chemistry Sets, new games and dolls, or a pretty dress from the City of Paris. Of course, all wrapping paper was saved for next year, long before recycling became popular.

The presents I gave were all handmade by me: potholders, clay pin dishes, soap carvings, drawings, pencil holders and decorated garden stakes from sixth grade Manual Training class. We had presents for our pets, too — catnip mice and cans of tuna for the cats, a ball or chewing toy for Nero. And there had to be small gifts for relatives or neighbors who stopped by, bringing homemade jelly or candy or fruitcake and getting some of Gargo's (my grandmother's) goodies in return.

Not all of our Christmas treats were made by Gargo. My father's older sister, Aunt Alma, who lived in San Diego, always sent a big box of goodies: guava jelly, candies, and special German cookies like *pfefferneuse* and *springerle*. She was married to a baker, Otto Reutinger, so I don't know which one of them made the cookies but they were delicious and left a satisfying powdered sugar dusting on ones lips and chin.

Packages arriving at our door were another exciting part of Christmas. My grandmother had left many dear friends and relations in the East and in Pasadena where she and my mother lived when they first came to California in 1910. So there were always packages from Cousin Jessie, Cousin Mabel or Aunt Alice, they usually turned out, disappointingly for me, to be silk stockings, linen handkerchiefs or lilac scented sachets. One of the cousins always sent a subscription to the Readers' Digest which I enjoyed reading even though my parents ridiculed it.

Quite a few gifts arrived for my father, too, but they were a sort of joke — appreciation or solicitation gifts from various contractors or building supply companies for using their services or materials. There was a serving tray, depicting a goose flying over woods with a full moon above and my parents names inscribed below it. It wasn't their style at all but we used it for years because it was sturdy and just the right size for tea time or invalid meals. Then there was a set of good steak knives, which I still use, paper weights of sample materials and sometimes a bottle of good whiskey which my father enjoyed, especially a dollop in his coffee occasionally.

After all the presents were open, we had a big Christmas dinner, though not necessarily turkey which was more for Thanksgiving dinner, an adult occasion to which my parents invited a few friends and neighborhood loners. Then came a walk in the hills and visits to and from neighbors and, finally, time to savor my new possessions.

Christmas is still my favorite holiday in spite of the cynical, antireligious, anticapitalist shells I have grown to protect my secretly sentimental core — the shameful part of me that cries at "Lassie" movies and high school graduation ceremonies. I have learned to avoid, ignore or laugh at the excesses of decoration, advertising, compulsive buying and maudlin sentimentality. Christmas is my celebration of family and friends, of glorious music, of the turning of the seasons, of love and hope and peace. I seem to have passed my fondness for this celebration on to my children and grandchildren for we always come together at this time to share our giving and our lives.

MORE CELEBRATIONS

Next to Christmas, I liked Halloween best. I was encouraged to have a few friends over to bob for apples and to roast chestnuts and marshmallows in the fireplace. We usually had hot cider, too. I don't remember much fuss about costumes. We wrapped up in a sheet or wore oversized old clothes to be hoboes and then went out to haunt the neighborhood. There were no treats then, just tricks. My favorite tricks were soaping the windows of cars parked along the street or ringing doorbells and running away to hide and giggle when the baffled (we thought) residents came to the door. If I felt especially daring, I might leave someone's garden hose running or stick a pin in a doorbell button so it would keep ringing. To someone like me who was almost always a good girl these seemed like very naughty things to do and I found the feeling exhilarating.

Of course, we always had a least one hand-carved jack-o'-lantern. I loved the whole process of creating it: picking out just the right size and shape of pumpkin, spreading out newspapers on the kitchen table, cutting out the top of the pumpkin, then scooping and scraping out all the stringy, slimy yellow pulp and little pale seeds which tended to stick to the sides if I wasn't careful. The smell of the pulp was strong and sharp and clung to my hands even after I had washed them. The skin of my hands felt dry and stretched. Then I would draw on the face with a black grease pencil and carve it very carefully, occasion-

I requestd a black baby doll. (This is Berkeley.)

Rosalie, Father and Nero, 1929.

Helena, Mother, Rosalie, 1927.

Elizabeth, Helena, Gargo, Rosalie, 1930.

ally cutting off a tooth unintentionally. Deciding what kind of face to draw was hard. As I got older, I thought the traditional smiling face was too childish and I liked to make sad or scary ones with jagged teeth or crossed eyes. Getting the candle to stick to the bottom was tricky. One had to cut a little depression in the bottom of the pumpkin, drip some melted wax into it, and then set the candle firmly in the wax before it hardened. Often we had one jack-o'-lantern shining out the living room window and another on the stair post out by the public walk to greet the tricksters. The jack-o'-lanterns stayed there until their faces caved in from thick green mold, and that was interesting to watch, too.

Easter was our spring celebration and all four females in the family helped to decorate the eggs, though the older I got the more I was allowed to do. Decorating was a ritual like pumpkin carving, starting with boiling the eggs and waiting in suspense to see how many would crack. Then came the newspapers, the little cups, one for each color of dye, the spoons for dipping the eggs and the empty egg cartons for drying them, plus the crayons and decals we used for special effects. There was always the smell of vinegar that was supposed to make the dye take better.

My grandmother and mother hid the eggs in the garden, usually near the lawn or one of the terraces or paths so we wouldn't trample too many plants while hunting. They had to hide them not long before the Hunt so the dogs or slugs didn't get to them first. If I ever believed a bunny left the eggs, I don't remember it. The only candy my sister and I got was a chocolate rabbit and some yellow marshmallow chicks at our places at breakfast. I could make the rabbit last a day or two by nibbling a little at a time but the chicks were gone in a few hours.

For Easter we had store-bought baskets and curly paper grass, but for May Day it was tradition to weave baskets out of strips of colored construction paper. We filled the baskets with many kinds of flowers from the garden and left them on the doorsteps of our favorite neighbors. Maybe that was our atonement for Halloween pranks!

The big summer holiday, of course, was the Fourth of July. There were no safety laws then, but we were expected to treat fireworks with caution and respect. We had long strings of firecrackers from Chinatown and boxes full of sparklers, both of which we were allowed to light unsupervised by the time I was six or so (the firecrackers one at a time.) We had to light them on the lawn or one of the open terraces where the fire hazard was least, but I did get a few singed fingers and a blistered heel when I stepped barefoot on an expired but still hot sparkler. After that I wore shoes and didn't throw used sparklers on the ground. The pops, bangs, whines and sizzles started in the neighborhood a day or two before the Fourth and I wanted to join in the noisemaking. The night of the Fourth was the big show, of course. My parents would have purchased Roman Candles, Pin Wheels, rockets and all the prettiest displays available and the neighbor kids would gather on our lawn while one of the adults in my family set off the show. I loved the suspense of waiting to find out what shapes and colors we would see, how long each one would last or whether it would be a dud. Everyone oohed, aahed or groaned. If something didn't go off, we had the added suspense of waiting to see if it would explode when an adult went to relight it. I liked the big colored pinwheels and the cascades of sparks better than the loud bangs.

This show lasted about a half-hour and then we went up to the top of the tower to watch the spectacular displays down by the waterfront and across the Bay. Now the big displays are all that's left of the Fourth of July.

Early Crimes

With three adults and a much older sister to keep me in line, I was usually a model of good behavior. But there were times when small acts of rebellion, dishonesty or meanness seeped through the cracks in my saintly façade.

I think I was about eight when I stole the diamond ring. I was allowed to walk, by myself, the six blocks or so down the hill to Telegraph Avenue (in those days it was perfectly safe) to spend my ten-cents weekly allowance at the Golden Bear Variety Store there. Mostly, I spent it on candy corn or red hots or Necco Wafers, but sometimes I found a tiny doll or toy or other trinket for ten cents. The dime store was small, two aisles with a center display counter. Usually there was only one clerk, reading by the cash register, as it was never crowded. The place had an odd sweet but musty smell unique to dime stores of that era. On this day, the center counter had a display of fake jewelry, clear and colored glass bead necklaces and rings and I was drawn to a large, sparkly diamond ring, about the size of a plump blueberry. It cost 25 cents. I wandered up and down the aisles, first on one side of the counter, then on the other, examining things as I went and fingering the ring which lay loose in a section of other rings. My desire for that ring became overwhelming, and when I saw the clerk still engrossed in her book, I slipped the ring into my pocket. Then I picked out some candy, paid for it with my dime and left my heart pounding. A block away and seemingly safe, I put the ring on my finger and admired it all the way back up the hill.

That evening my grandmother and I started playing our usual game of Russian Bank when she noticed the ring on my hand and questioned me about it. I was not a good liar and soon the truth was out, as I must have known it would be. It took but little scolding from Gargo for me to feel deeply ashamed. The next day after school, Gargo accompanied me to the variety store while I returned the ring and apologized to the clerk. I never shoplifted again, ever.

Another serious breach of honesty involved plagiarism. I liked to write poems and little stories for a children's column in the Berkeley Daily Gazette called the Young Author's Club and run by an "Aunt Flo." My efforts had appeared in the paper several times and reaped me a lot of praise. There was to be a poetry contest and I wanted to win it but I felt I needed a little help. The poem I was writing was about the garden after a rain and I found some lines in a book of poetry by Eugene Field, I think about pansies with muddy faces and other pretty images of wet flowers. A couple of stanzas fit very well into what I wanted to say. Apparently, Aunt Flo didn't recognize the lines because the poem appeared in the paper and I did win a prize (though I can't remember what it was.) But my mother recognized the stanzas; she had probably read them to me when I was much younger, and I got a lecture that made me feel like the thief I was. After that I don't think I even copied anyone else's homework.

Sometimes I was naughty just to be mean. One of my chores, which I really enjoyed, was to walk the half mile or so up Strawberry Canyon to the University's Poultry Experiment Station where we bought our eggs because they were said to be extra fresh and nutritious. I took a small basket to carry the eggs home in, as egg cartons were not provided. The Poultry Station was managed by a family named Mugglestone (whose English name I thought ridiculous) and I sometimes played with their daughter Margaret. There were probably more than two hundred chickens and the whole place had the dusty, sour smell of chicken manure and the constant sound of clucks, cackles and crows. The narrow, dirt road, closed to cars, which I followed to the Station went past the University Men's Swimming Pool and often I would linger at the chain link fence and watch the young men diving or racing. It was a lovely location for a pool, ringed by the oak and bay trees along Strawberry Creek, and it seemed unfair that women weren't allowed there.

One time, on my way back home with my basket of two dozen eggs, I found the pool deserted. It lay flat and still, without a ripple. On impulse, I took an egg and lofted it over the six foot fence and into the pool, creating satisfying concentric circles in the water. I suppose it sank to the bottom without breaking, but I hoped some show-off college boy would step on it and get an unpleasant surprise. I wanted to throw another egg onto the concrete pool deck and watch it splatter, but I thought that would be too mean. And besides, my grandmother might notice if there were two eggs missing.

My other major crime in those years involved destruction of property. I was being punished for some infraction of rules and had to spend an hour or so shut up in my grandmother's bedroom. I don't remember what I had done wrong but I was feeling really resentful about the punishment. Gargo had a nice wood sewing cabinet with a bin on each side to hold yarn or scraps of cloth and four drawers in front for sewing notions. Each drawer had two little wooden knobs for handles. I took a pin and scratched the finish of that cabinet, carefully gouging across the front of each drawer and around each knob. Of course, my vandalism was discovered soon after I was let out of prison, but I don't remember what my punishment for that was. The sewing cabinet was passed down through the generations and now belongs to my younger daughter. No one ever refinished it so my scratches are still visible to remind me of my youthful crime.

Early Music

I can't remember when music was not an important part of my life. By the time I was three, my sister was practicing the piano daily and soon started on the violin as well. When my mother put me to bed, she would often sing to me Brahms' *Lullaby* or the Slumber Song from *Hansel and Gretel* or *Speed, Bonnie Boat*.

Every weekend we listened to the Metropolitan Opera and the New York Philharmonic broadcasts. For weekdays we had an Edison phonograph, built into a handsome carved and decorated Chinese cabinet behind the piano, at the end of the living room. We had thick albums of fat, one-sided records of Beethoven symphonies, Mozart concertos, Wagnerian overtures, Brahms, Bach and most of the Greats. I think the adults would have played them more if they hadn't had to be right there to change the record every few minutes. We also had songs by artists like Enrico Caruso, Paul Robeson and John Charles Thomas (who?) but I didn't like those as much as the orchestral music. Reportedly, I announced when I was three-and-half or four that my favorite piece was Beethoven's Fifth. (Of course, by then I knew something about winning adult approval.)

My sister, Helena, was musically talented and her piano renditions of Chopin etudes and Beethoven sonatas earned her a lot of praise and attention. I wanted to get in on that, so when I was four I asked to have piano lessons. My mother arranged for a young woman teacher to come to the house and get me started on scales and exercises. I had one of those charts that stand up behind the piano keys and tell you what note you are playing and, of course, I knew my letters.

I practiced faithfully for several years but it became apparent to me that I could never catch up to my sister. She was always asked to play for company (if not, she offered), and after her virtuoso performance I would be asked to play one of the simple ditties I had mastered: *The Happy Farmer* or *Twinkle, Twinkle*. I took to disappearing quietly and hiding in a closet or under a bed so I wouldn't have to play. At least once, my mother, after calling me repeatedly, came and found me, coaxed me out from under the bed and insisted I perform. I don't know whether she thought it was good social training for me or whether she couldn't bear to have Helena, her stepdaughter, get so much more attention than me, her biological daughter.

I kept practicing, with increasing reluctance, for the next ten years. When I was about twelve and my sister was eighteen, she had a prospective boyfriend who lived in the apartment across the walk and who also played the piano. They would play to each other, often Beethoven's Moonlight Sonata as a romantic dialogue back and forth across the walk. I wanted to be part of that so I learned the first, slow movement of the sonata and when I was ready, I played it at a time when I knew the young man was at home. I was thrilled to have him answer me on his piano, but he went on to the second, fast *appassionato* movement, which was beyond my skills. I had to give up, revealing myself as a phony and a poor substitute.

For a few months I tried the violin while my sister was going to school in Europe again and my playing couldn't be compared with hers. But I found it much harder than the piano, so I went back to that and a series of patient teachers until I finally rebelled at age fourteen. My mother and grandmother tried to coax me into keeping on with lessons, telling me how much I would regret stopping and saying I could switch to popular music. They tried to paint a rosy picture of me playing at teenage parties, surrounded by admiring friends who would sing to my accompaniment. I tried a few lessons, but was put off by *Chiribiribin* or whatever the teacher considered popular then. I wanted to sound like Duke Ellington or forget it. I've never been sorry I quit.

Besides listening to music at home, we went to a lot of local concerts mostly free chamber music or solo performances at the University. Evening or wet-weather concerts were generally held in Wheeler Hall on campus, though if something really big came to town like the Don Cossack Chorus, the old Phoebe A. Hearst gym became the concert hall. I didn't much enjoy concerts at Wheeler. It was crowded and stuffy and hard to see and I had to sit still. Often, I got sleepy.

But I did enjoy going to concerts and plays at the Greek Theater, which was only a few blocks from our house. In the summer, a series of Sunday afternoon performances was held there, called the *Half Hour of Music*. Most of the artists were minor local ones who would perform free and my father referred to these concerts as the *Hour of Half Music*. But I enjoyed walking there, around the football stadium and into the grove of aromatic eucalyptus that surrounded the Theater. The broad concrete benches were very hard so we brought cushions and usually a lap robe if the fog was coming in. We sat way up in the back where there weren't many people, so before and after a concert I got to run along the tiers of benches, jumping across the aisles, and up and down the stairs. Gargo liked to get one of the throne-like concrete seats down in front, so as to have support for her back. I tried sitting with her because it looked important but I found I was too easily noticed and had to sit still just like in Wheeler Hall. Up in the back I had a lot more freedom to move around, swing my feet, look at the clouds, smell the eucalyptus and listen to the blue jays, who didn't know they were supposed to be quiet.

I'm not sure how much these afternoons did for my musical development. I always loved big symphonies and later, big choral works. But I didn't come to appreciate chamber music until I was almost 60, and I am still not fond of solo singing or instrumental works. My joy in college and for most of the past 20 years has been singing in a large chorus.

Now the Greek Theater is used for huge rock concerts. The whole area is clogged with traffic, parking is almost impossible and the residents of Panoramic Hill are kept awake until late at night by the powerfully-amplified sounds. Recently I saw a T-shirt for a rock band that performed there, with a background of the campanile and the Golden Gate Bridge and the message "Groovin' at the Greek."

Summer Fun
Camp Fire Camp

When I was about ten and longing to be part of a group of girls, my mother and grandmother urged me to join the Camp Fire Girls rather than the Girl Scouts. In liberal Berkeley circles, even back then, the Scouts had a reputation for being over regimented, even slightly fascistic. A friend of the family, Augusta Trumpler, who was also the mother of my friend Liz, was forming a Camp Fire group to meet at her house, a convenient distance for me between school and my house farther up the hill. There were about eight of us girls who met weekly in Mrs. Trumpler's dining room to work on beaded headbands and buckskin colored heavy cotton ceremonial robes with fake leather fringe and to learn the Camp Fire precepts embodied in the ritual word "WoHeLo" (WorkHealthLove). We didn't take it too seriously and we still had time for games and art projects like Christmas cards, soap carving, spatter prints and place mats woven with strips of colored paper. It was a lively time and probably the first time I ever felt like a member of a group. Mrs. Trumpler's four other children, Liz's two older sisters and two younger brothers, kept coming in and out of the room, and rapid fire French or German flew back and forth between the family members. Mrs. T. was French Swiss and Professor T. was German Swiss so both languages were spoken, on alternate days or weeks, to keep the children in practice. I thought it was a wonderful family with so many children and so many activities and I wished my family were more like that.

When summertime came there was much talk of Going to Camp and though I was fearful I determined to do it. it. Camp Celio was only a few hours away, in the foothills near Grass Valley, and we would be taken there by bus. (My family still had no car.) Soon we got the lists of gear and clothing to take. My mother had an old lambs wool and khaki sleeping bag, left over from Sierra Club days, but we had to go buy the royal blue shirts and shorts with a white set for Sundays. Everything had to be marked with sewn on red embroidered name tapes, which Gargo went right to work on.

The day of departure came and I watched scornfully, my stomach in a cold, hard knot, as many of the girls cried while boarding the bus and saying goodbye to their mothers. Camp Celio was situated on pine covered hills beside a small artificial lake. It was warm and bright when we arrived and the pine and bay and coyote brush smelled wonderful. There was a big lodge made of logs and two groups of tent cabins, one for the elementary school girls and another farther away on a different hill for junior high and up. Though I was not quite eleven, I had had a semester of junior high so I was put in the older girls' camp. I was miserable; my tent mates talked about clothes, hairstyles, boys, lipstick, brassieres, and which counselor was the cutest. I was nowhere near ready for that. My understanding counselor agreed to take me to see the camp director, an athletic looking hawk-eyed woman who listened to my plea to be put in the camp where my sixth grade friends were. She told me if I was in the seventh grade I should be like the seventh graders, but she agreed to phone my mother and discuss the situation. My mother must have given permission for me to be "demoted" because by nighttime I was settled in the younger kids camp with tent mates who made me feel much more comfortable.

After that, I had fun. I improved my swimming skills

enough to pass the Junior Red Cross "Frog" level, learned to canoe, went on hikes and nature study outings, worked on craft projects made out of pine cones, needles, bark, wildflowers and grasses and got pretty good at archery. Evenings were campfire times and we listened to spooky owls and ghost stories and learned many songs, some of which I loved and some of which I thought stupid. The one about Remembering Camp Celio was particularly corny and helped the older girls cry on cue. Crying was not done in my household except when my mother or grandmother had a tantrum and I found it very strange that these girls seemed to like to cry. They also liked to giggle hysterically and one very popular fourteen year old laughed so hard she wet her pants right in front of a bunch of her friends, then just laughed about that! I would have felt utterly disgraced.

 The climax of our two week stay was an Overnight Hike for which we had to do a great deal of planning and preparation. Our sleeping and cooking gear and extra clothes were transported by pickup truck to a spot about five miles distant where we would spend the night. We carried just our lunches and water in our knapsacks and had a leisurely walk through the woods and along a rushing flume. Our counselor led the way, carrying a forked stick to pin down possible rattlers so we were all on the alert for that heart-chilling buzz but we never heard anything more dangerous than a cicada. Our gear was all there when we arrived and that night we learned to make biscuits on a stick and roast corn to go with our hotdogs. The biscuits were tricky as the dough tended to slide off the stick into the fire or get burnt on the outside while still raw inside, but we didn't care. Dessert was s'mores, of course, another wonderfully messy concoction of toasted marshmallow and melting Hershey square on a graham cracker. I had slept out on the lawn at home, but I was thrilled to be sleeping outside in this strange place, surrounded by friendly protectors as I listened to the soft mysterious night sounds and tried to see into the deep shadows, with millions of stars overhead.

When it was time to board the bus to return to Berkeley, there were a lot more tears, even among the girls whose parents came in cars to pick them up. I thought this whole scene pretty silly and somewhat insulting to the parents and I remained stony faced. Though I returned to Camp Celio for four more summers and got to be one of the Big Girls who wore lipstick and brassieres, fussed with my hair, had a crush on my counselor and worried about bloodstains on the seat of my white shorts, I never did cry when I left. The last summer, when I was almost fifteen, my sister, who was twenty-one, had a job as counselor at the YWCA camp right next door. We would meet by the fence between the campgrounds to chat or show off what we had done and occasionally we visited each other's camps. Helena had a boyfriend, of course, a counselor from a nearby boys' camp, so she didn't have a lot of time for me but I think having her there gained some status for me in the eyes of my peers. The summer after that I finished high school early by going to summer school and suddenly I was enrolling at UC Berkeley and no longer felt like a child who went to camp.

Piano Lessons, Ages four to fourteen.

Nero, Mother and Rosalie

With Dünkel, my 18 pound cat.

My favorite baby doll, Marjorie.

Summer Fun
The Ranch

I loved summertime; life felt so much freer then. I could spend lots of time outdoors, away from adult supervision and adult tensions. One place we visited quite often was a ranch in Sonoma County near the Russian River. It belonged to an old flame of my mother, a man who had been the University of California medalist but whose doctor had told him that in order to preserve his health he should live a quiet life in the country. He had married a Vassar girl who was in my mother's circle of acquaintances and whom my mother considered (quite rightly) to be much less attractive than herself. (This woman, whom my sister and I called "Aunt Frances," was much less volatile and more manageable than my mother.) She and "Uncle Rene" had a dairy and chicken farm in Windsor. They also had two daughters, one a couple of years older, the other a couple of years younger than myself. They lived in an old-fashioned farmhouse with a big kitchen-family room, a formal parlor, and attic bedrooms reached by narrow, creaky stairs. The bedrooms were supplied with commodes and water pitchers because the only bathroom was downstairs. There was a big screen porch along the front of the house where we three girls slept on summer nights and a smaller back porch, which was the mudroom and storage area. It wasn't anything like my house in Berkeley and I liked the differentness of it.

Often it was just my mother and myself who went on these visits, my sister either being away at school or too much older to want to come along. My father, also, usually stayed at home doing the work he said he had to catch up on (but never did). I suppose my mother and Aunt Frances chatted about the vicissitudes of marriage and child rearing while I played with the two girls. For a while I was better friends with the older sister (also named Frances but called Fran) but when she entered adolescence and I was still far from it I turned to the younger, Cynthia, as my playmate and confidante. By then, the family had built a little guest cottage, complete with bunk beds, where we could hang out in privacy. We got to feed the chickens, gather the eggs, watch the cows being milked and the bull in action when it was time for him to do his job. We also fed and petted the heifers out in the fields, picked wild blackberries and fresh vegetables from Frances Sr.'s garden and helped to prepare them for supper, watched the daily train pass along the eastern boundary of the ranch, inspected the chick incubator with its fluffy, peeping inhabitants, or the various machines for pasteurizing milk or separating cream. Also in the barnyard were the big tractor, disker and other farm machinery we could climb up on.

 The cows were all named for relatives or friends of the family, a practice which my family found silly and slightly insulting, but I rather enjoyed getting to know my namesake a soft-eyed cream and white Jersey. Fran had a heifer she had raised which would allow her to ride on its back for short periods a very strange sight I thought. There was a small chicken coop inside a fence and away from the main chicken houses that was an infirmary and isolation ward for the chickens. I was both intrigued and repelled by watching these sickly creatures with filmed eyes or odd growths or missing feathers who gave mournful croaking or burbling cries very unlike the busy, noisy clucks and crows of the healthy chickens. The young pullets were allowed to run free during the day and wandered, pecking and scratching over the grassy fields and under the old oak trees. The oaks attracted redheaded acorn woodpeckers, birds we didn't see at home in Berkeley, and I loved to hear their calls and watch their flashing flight. Once I witnessed a farmland drama when I saw a wandering pullet grabbed and carried off by a circling red-tailed hawk. For a city child like myself, the ranch was a wonderland.

Our favorite play places were the barn and the creek. The barn was filled with bales of hay, up to the roof in places, but with plenty of spaces for hide-and-go-seek, climbing and jumping and for swinging way out on a long rope, then dropping into a soft, scratchy, sneezy pile of loose hay. We couldn't play in there while the cows were being milked because the noise might make them nervous and "curdle the milk" but the rest of the time the barn was ours. The creek that ran through the ranch was just right for children to play in — not enough water to be dangerous but enough to float our homemade boats and to lend itself to dam building and other engineering feats. It was also a cool, shady place on hot summer days.

Both the creek and the barn were neglected, though, after the girls got ponies. Then, taking turns if necessary, we would go galloping across the fields, being knights and crusaders more often than cowboys and Indians. The summer I was twelve I went to the ranch and was devastated to find that the ponies had been sold and the girls had a horse. They brought him up from the barn for me to inspect and he looked to me to be twenty feet high. I was afraid of anything more than six feet off the ground but the girls and their parents kept urging me to get aboard, assuring me it was a very gentle horse. When I finally got settled in the saddle, the horse took off at a good clip down the hill toward the barn. It was less than a quarter of a mile but I had no control over the beast and he knew it, so I simply clung to the saddle horn, terrified that I would fall off and be paralyzed for life. The horse stopped when it got to the barn and gave me a superior shimmy as I slid shakily to the ground. I never rode that horse again and have only once or twice mounted any other — and then with great reluctance.

By the time of the horse incident, Fran was already much involved in high school, 4H activities and boys. As Cynthia and I grew into adolescence (she matured before I did though she was more than two years younger) we saw less and less of the family and of the ranch. Fran came to college at UC Berkeley and roomed with me in our house while she studied music, fell in love and got married. Cynthia married at seventeen to an older man and quickly produced three children. Frances and Rene divorced after (but not because) Frances had an affair with the local dentist. The ranch was sold and the family scattered. When I went back recently to try to find my old Wonderland, there seemed to be no farmland left; condos and mobile home parks had taken over and shopping malls were building.

Summer Fun
Carmel by the Sea

In the early 1930's, Carmel was not the tourist town it is today. It was a haven for artists, writers, free-thinkers and bohemians, and a summer vacation spot for those attracted to its liberal atmosphere as well as its scenic beauty.

When my mother started working full time in 1930, my grandmother became responsible for my summer care and entertainment. Gargo loved the arty, intellectual yet small-town atmosphere of Carmel. For several years, before she bought a house there, she would rent a cottage for as long as two months in the summer and take me with her. My sister was usually involved in teen activities elsewhere and my parents were working, so it was just Gargo and me.

Our family didn't own a car until 1937, so Gargo and I would catch the Del Monte Express from San Francisco to Monterey, then a local bus on to Carmel and a taxi to wherever our rented cottage was located. Some of these cottages were much more attractive than others, but they all belonged to the Carmel Quaint style of architecture. None was very close to the beach because those were far too expensive, but we were used to doing a lot of walking up and down the Berkeley Hills. The place I liked best looked more New England than Carmel. It was white board and batten with dark green trim and a small colorful garden edged with abalone shells and was part of a court of six cottages called the Sherwood Forest Cabins. Ours was Friar Tuck. It had a fireplace for foggy mornings and evenings and was only a few blocks from the beach, though more than a mile from grocery stores and the Post Office.

Nielson Brothers Grocery would deliver Gargo's telephone orders, but I walked to the village almost every day to get the mail and to do simple errands. Gargo walked with me if she thought any transaction would be too difficult for me, but I enjoyed going alone as it made me feel more important. It was fun to get to know the dogs along the way (most of them were friendly) and to peer into all the different gardens and front windows. Backyards were interesting, too; you could tell a lot about a family by the clothes hanging on the line, the toys and bikes left out and the discards by the back door. I could pick my own route from the grid of streets with names like Dolores, Junipero Serra, El Camino, Monte Verde and Mission. (Somehow a street named Lincoln got mixed in there.) I memorized all the names of the north south streets and then the east west ones and could recite them in order, though I could never remember all the state capitals. It was nine blocks north and six blocks east up the hill to the Post Office where everyone had to come to get mail, as there was no home delivery. The area around the Post Office was always crowded with cars looking for parking places or blocking traffic as their drivers chatted with friends. It was a lively scene which I enjoyed observing.

Gargo thought it was ridiculous to make everyone go to the Post Office, especially in summer when there were so many vacationers there. The P.O. wouldn't deliver then unless there were sidewalks for the safety of the mail carriers (this was before they even had pushcarts), and the town fathers and regular residents didn't want to put in sidewalks because that would spoil the rustic village look so many people loved. Another reason I liked going to town was to window-shop the stores full of interesting and expensive *objets d'art* but mostly to browse the library and the variety store. I bought a lot of Shirley Temple paper dolls, balsa wood gliders, marbles, yoyos and candy there.

I rarely had a playmate in Carmel so I spent a lot of time alone at the beach or exploring the rocks and tide pools. Gargo couldn't swim and since I could, I think she figured I would be safe. She had no idea of the danger of waves and currents and undertow though she always warned me to be careful. I was a pretty cautious child, but I remember several times I got rolled in the surf and came up gasping or had to fight the current out beyond the breakers. I was not a strong swimmer but I managed somehow to get back to shore.

Sometimes Gargo would come with me and we would have a picnic lunch. She loved watching the waves and the shore birds and pelicans, but she sunburned badly and had to stay completely covered up, not even taking off her shoes and stockings to wade. She also disliked sitting on rocks or sand with no back support (there were no aluminum folding chairs then). I didn't understand her discomfort then, but I do now!

Of course, I made sand castles and drawings, collected shells and kelp to decorate them, captured and released sand crabs to see how fast they could burrow back down, whipped imaginary enemies with long kelp bullwhips or jumped rope with shorter pieces and delighted in stepping on the dry kelp bulbs so they would pop loudly. I learned how to catch a wave and ride it in a kind of early body surfing, I guess. And I didn't mind fog or cold weather. I remember swimming, though briefly, one time when we were there for Thanksgiving!

Besides the long curve of white sand beach, Carmel has another beach where the Carmel River meets the sea. In summer, a sandbar forms across the mouth of the river, making a safe, shallow lagoon for quiet paddling or boat launching. But on the ocean side of the sand bar the coarse yellow sand beach drops off very steeply, the undertow is frightening and waves enormous — building all the way in from Point Lobos. I knew better than to swim there. The River Beach is separated from the Main Beach by rocky cliffs and flats known as "The Point" where the tide pools, at least in those days, were rich with sea creatures. I could spend hours watching, poking at and rearranging hermit crabs, rock crabs, snails and starfish. Barnacles, limpets and anemones are not rearrangeable and sea urchins are very tricky to relocate but anemones are a lot of fun to make close up and squirt. I soon learned that the starfish and crabs didn't last long when brought home in a coffee can of sea water and the dead ones smelled terrible so I left them in their tide pools. Just watching the huge waves piling up and rushing toward the beach or crashing on the rocks was exciting. I was daring either the tide to come in and trap me or the waves to wash me away.

One summer I did find a playmate named Dawn who lived with her mother in a little house near the one we were renting. Gargo thought her not a very suitable playmate because her mother worked cleaning hotel rooms, but we had a lot of fun anyway. Dawn was a real tomboy; more daring than I was, except when it came to handling tide pool animals. She was a better swimmer, but I usually beat her at cards or board games. We didn't write to each other during the winter and when I returned to Carmel the next summer I was desolate to find that she and her mother had moved away.

There was plenty of opportunity for cultural enrichment in the town. Art and photo exhibits were all around, there were concerts in the mission or the school auditorium, plays in the Forest Theater where we sat outside wrapped in coats and blankets while fog drifted across the stage, and poetry readings in private homes. The most famous resident poet then was Robinson Jeffers who was just completing his castle-like, all stone Tor House, down on The Point. I walked by there often and once stepped onto his property to get a close look, but he poked his head out of one of the tower windows, shook his fist at me and yelled for me to get off the property. I didn't read any of his poetry for years after that.

The summer I was twelve and my sister was eighteen, she spent a month in Carmel with Gargo and me, practicing for and playing violin in the summer festival orchestra. Helena had curly blond hair, a sunny disposition and a way with the boys, so it wasn't long before she had a boyfriend from the orchestra walking her home after rehearsals. I was fascinated by this opportunity to observe firsthand a budding romance. One day the boyfriend (Carlo?) was invited to go to the beach with the rest of us. My grandmother came, too, but she was scandalized by the skimpiness of Helena's bathing suit and the way the two of them touched and rubbed oil on each other. Helena got a very sharp lecture and there were no more family invitations, but I'm sure she continued to see Carlo on her own. I filed this experience away for the future and when I was eighteen and singing in the Bach Festival Chorus in Carmel, my boyfriend picked me up after rehearsal and we went somewhere before returning to Gargo's cottage. I owed my sister a lot.

The most beautiful Fourth of July I ever saw was at Carmel Beach. Campfires and all kinds of fireworks were allowed, each family or group making its own display so that the whole two miles of white sand beach were lit up with fountains and pinwheels, Roman candles and starbursts, and by children writing their names or drawing pictures in the dark with sparklers. The knobby, windbent Monterey cypress on the cliff rimming the beach made weird dancing shadows in the exploding lights. It was like magic, but the trees are still there, sixty years later.

Summer Fun
Visiting Mt. Hamilton

For a while when I was small, Robert and Augusta Trumpler and their five children were our neighbors on Panoramic Way. Dr. Trumpler was an astronomer at UC and Mrs. Trumpler was the founding mother of the Berkeley Co-op, the force behind the Unitarian Church and the Women's International League for Peace and Freedom, and any other organization which interested her. The children were Alfred, two years younger than I, Robert who was my age but not my playmate, Elizabeth (called Doodie by her mother, much to her embarrassment) who was a year and a half older but in my grade, Margot, and then Cecile who was my sister's age and went on a trip to Europe with her and my grandmother. I was fascinated with this big, active, noisy family and wished mine could be more like it.

When Dr. Trumpler was sent to Mount Hamilton to be head of Lick Observatory, the whole family went along and we saw them only occasionally when they came to town or for special events or shopping and visiting. The women kept in touch but we couldn't visit, as we still didn't own a car. One time when Mrs. T. was in Berkeley and calling on my mother, she suggested I come back with her and spend a few days on Mt. Hamilton. I was about eight years old and had never spent a night away from home on my own, but I stifled my fears with the lure of being with that wonderful family and exploring a new place without my mother's overly careful supervision. She

OVERCOMING CHILDHOOD ADVANTAGES

was working full time by then and Gargo must have been in Europe with Helena so I needed some summer activity.

I was very excited and was all packed and waiting when Mrs. T. came to pick me up the next morning. I didn't get to ride in cars much so the drive itself was thrilling until we started climbing up the steep, winding dirt road from the valley to the top of Mt. Hamilton. The more curves we went around, the sicker I felt. When I was six I had disgraced myself by throwing up on the navy blue wool baize upholstery of Dr. and Mrs. Allen's new Buick as they drove us along Highway 9 to their cabin in Boulder Creek. This time I knew enough to ask Mrs. T. to stop, or maybe she noticed the green shade of my face — before the disaster happened. She told me to walk back and forth on the road and breathe deep and it helped — for a while. We must have stopped three or four times on our way up the mountain but I managed to keep my breakfast down.

The Trumpler's home was a big old-fashioned farmhouse type with plenty of comfortable clutter inside. The children greeted me happily and "Doodie" took me upstairs to see the bedroom I would share with her. There was a huge old oak tree outside the window and a view all the way down to the valley, but the nearby mountainside looked steep, dry and dusty — the grasses all a California summer tan. There was not enough water up there to waste on a lawn or flower garden.

Back downstairs in the kitchen Mrs. T. was taking out some icebox pudding she had made. She was very proud of having an electric refrigerator there; I guess it was more practical for the University than supplying ice in that remote spot. The pudding was pink and gelatinous and didn't appeal to my still queasy stomach. But Mrs. T. urged me to have some, telling me it was a delicious specialty of hers and would soothe my digestion. I tasted a little and it was horrible — it tasted like the oil my grandmother used on her sewing machine! — and

I couldn't eat it though the others seemed to like it all right. I must have turned green again because Mrs. T. kindly suggested I go outside for some fresh air. She implied that I was suffering from homesickness. Soon Doodie and the two brothers joined me and gave me a tour of the property. They had a swing set and bars, perched on the edge of the steep, dry hillside, but the big oak tree was the best climbing. It wasn't long before I began to feel better.

The next day we all got to go on a picnic to the Camp. This was a section of the grassy woodland covered with oak and madrone in a small ravine where a little creek still dribbled slowly. It was accessible only by scrambling down a steep hillside slippery with dry leaves, while dodging clumps of poison oak. There was enough flat land and enough water in the creek for the vegetable garden the family had planted nearby and there were plenty of children to haul the water. There was a badminton net and a rustic table and logs or stumps for seats. Sometimes the children brought their sleeping bags to camp out. To me it seemed a rather bare, uninteresting spot, but the family seemed to love it. I was warned to look out for rattlesnakes as well as poison oak, which didn't increase my affinity for the place. After lunch, we all picked vegetables and hauled them, along with all the picnic gear, back up the dry, slippery hill.

That night we went to the observatory to look through one of the telescopes. I had the idea I would be able to move the telescope around, like binoculars, to look at a lot of different stars, but it wasn't like that. We were led into a huge dome where there seemed to be a lot of machinery for moving and adjusting the big scope. Dr. Trumpler had spent a lot of time focusing the telescope on a certain star or planet — Mars, maybe — and all we could do was take turns squinting into the eyepiece and making awed sounds about the distant light. To me, it didn't seem like much of a way to spend your nights.

Looking up with my own eyes at the whole sweep of starry sky was more thrilling.

The only other interesting thing on Mt. Hamilton was the schoolhouse. I couldn't see how all eight grades could be taught in one room by one teacher. The Trumpler children made up at least half the enrollment and they were certainly smart and knew a lot, but I was sure they didn't learn it all in that school. (The next year, the two older girls, Margot and Cecile, came to live with my family so they could go to high school in Berkeley, and two years after that the whole family moved back to town.)

I never went alone again to Mt. Hamilton, though after my mother got a car in 1937 we made a few family trips there. When I was a Camp Fire Girl and Mrs. Trumpler was our leader, she took the group up for a camp out. We had to ride in the back of an old truck and I almost got sick again, but I kept breathing deep and made it OK. I had more fun with the Camp Fire Girls than when I went on my own!

Public Appearances

When I was six, my school started an after-hours class in French and my mother saw to it that I was enrolled. It was a small class, maybe ten or twelve first-to-third graders, and I enjoyed it. We sat around informally in one of the empty classrooms and learned how to make strange sounds and speak words that outsiders couldn't understand. It was my first experience with a foreign language and I discovered it was like learning a secret code. We learned the names of many things, memorized poems and sang songs like *Frere Jacques* and *Sur le Pont d'Avignon.*

Near the end of the term, our teacher told us that we were invited to be in a performance in San Francisco, a gathering of all the French students and teachers in the area to show off their progress. We were each to memorize a poem or song in French to present to the audience. I don't remember what poem I was given to learn; it was probably no more than two or three stanzas and not difficult to memorize, but I was terrified of saying it in from of an audience.

The day of the performances arrived and we were transported to a big, musty old building in the City and ushered upstairs and into the backstage area of the auditorium. We had to wait there a long time, being very quiet and listening to the voices of other French students, large and small, doing their turn on stage. There was a great deal of clapping between numbers so we knew there was a big audience. I felt trapped back there, behind the heavy, dusty smelling curtains with the lights glaring harshly on the scuffed but shiny wood floors. My heart kept beating faster and harder. I had a hard time staying still and I was afraid I was going to throw up. When my turn came, my teacher pushed me gently but firmly out onto the stage. I was all alone up there with thousands of faces staring up at me. I wanted to just disappear, but I somehow managed to say my poem in a shaky voice and get back offstage. There was reassuring clapping and my teacher told me I did fine, but I knew I never again wanted to be alone on a stage.

We all got prizes from the French Society that arranged the performances. Mine was a thick book, for adults, on the adventures of polar explorer Roald Amundsen — in French. I couldn't read any of it and I was so disappointed that I didn't try to learn any more French until I was a junior in high school.

My other public appearance in those early years was much more enjoyable. My mother enrolled me in a tap dancing class at the Berkeley Women's City Club where I was also learning to swim. I think I was about eight. My parents considered ballet too rigid an art form and I was supposed to be too awkward for the Isadora Duncan type of Eurhythmics which my sister was so good at, but I did have a good sense of rhythm. I loved my black patent leather tap shoes and learning to tap dance the routines. We practiced on the stage of the City Club auditorium, which was smaller and less daunting than the one in San Francisco, and I soon felt right at home there.

We were to be a part of a program put on by various music and dance classes at the Club, the audience consisting of friends and relations. The number for our class of little girls was something to do with a daisy chain and we all had to have costumes made from the same pattern. Gargo went right to work and created an outfit I thought was lovely: green cotton shorts and a scoop neck white blouse with embroidered daisies and appliqueed all around the neck. Then there was a wreath for my head of the same kind of daisies. My family teased me gently about how silly the costume was, but I felt pretty in it anyway. I was good at tap dancing and I didn't miss a step during the performance. The costume and the other girls protected me from stage fright. I felt fine about that, even though I knew that tap dancing was not in the same cultural class as piano recitals or modern dance. It was something all my own that my sister didn't know how to do.

OVERCOMING CHILDHOOD ADVANTAGES

Guardian of Small Animals — Nero

Hiking companion — Nero

Helena and Nero, 1936

The Road to Wellness

I had a lot of colds and sinus infections when I was in elementary school. This worried my mother who (I thought) would have preferred a child with perfect health. I also frequently got nasty boils, particularly under my knees where the skin was worn and grubby from going round and round on the playground bars.

Our doctor and his family were neighbors and lukewarm friends. They lived in a house on top of Panoramic Hill and had the only tennis courts around. The twin boys were a little older than I, the girl a little younger and they all played tennis like pros. I tried to learn the game but was hopelessly uncoordinated. Even the college girl my mother hired to teach me gave up on me. So I never got chummy with the doctor's children, but their parents occasionally invited my parents to social gatherings and Dr. Hoyt always addressed them by their first names.

My mother was very impressed with Dr. Hoyt — maybe because she had wanted to be an M.D. but was persuaded her health wasn't strong enough (probably by some male chauvinist advisor). Sometimes she made mildly disparaging remarks about Mrs. Hoyt, who had been a nurse and whom the doctor had married "to help put him through medical school." Often Mother managed to get off work to take me to see Dr. Hoyt about my various respiratory and skin infections. His office was in a building on the fourth floor at Telegraph and Channing and the waiting room featured potted ferns, a goldfish tank, National Geographics and medicinal odors. Also, a nurse, Miss Sommers, who had a beaky nose, tightly pulled back grey hair under her starched white cap and coke bottle glasses. I didn't mind sitting in the waiting room as much as I did riding up in the elevator. There was a very old man in a maroon colored uniform who was the elevator operator and when he would ask what floor we wanted my mother always said, "Fowah" instead of "Four," which made me cringe. (She had been in California for twenty years.)

Dr. Hoyt decided that my infection came from a sort of autointoxication and that I could build up my resistance by being exposed to a diluted culture of my own germs — a very modern idea in the 1920's. He had his lab grow a culture from the germs in my nose and produced a thick, yellow, pus like substance with a sharp medicinal tang that was kept in a glass dish in the office refrigerator. I went for a treatment two or three times a week. As I sat on the examining table, my legs dangling, Miss Sommers would take some long, skinny strips of gauze, soak them in the yellow glop, then pack them way up my nose till my tears ran. I had to sit there for about half an hour with this stuff up my nose; then Miss Sommers came back and pulled the strips out slowly, one at a time, like long yellow and white tapeworms. It was disgusting and made my nose hurt and tickle but it didn't cure my sinus infections. Those stopped when I reached puberty, as many childhood afflictions do. I stopped having boils when I went to junior high where there were no bars to swing from. (Bars were for little kids.)

The other treatment Dr. Hoyt tried for me (or in order to get my mother off his back) was to recommend that I go to Sunshine School. This was a special school, run by the Berkeley School District, for children who were thought to be at some health risk. There were sunbaths, rest periods, a carefully balanced diet with healthful snacks, gentle exercise and a program to accommodate various mild afflictions. A doctor's recommendation was needed to get in and most students seemed to be skinny kids from the poorer sections of Berkeley. The school was held in a few rooms of the old McKinley School, which now housed administrative offices for the District. There were no other children there and the echoing halls and mostly empty play-yard felt creepy. The next year the school was moved to some portables at Thousand Oaks School, all the way across town and I had a long streetcar ride each way. It was the end of the line, just beyond Solano and the Alameda, and often the streetcar would be sitting there after school, waiting for its return passengers, and we got to help the motorman flip the woven seat backs so they faced the other way while he moved his tiller and cash box to the other end of the car.

I had my first real crush on a teacher in the fifth grade at Sunshine School. Mrs. Evans looked quite a bit like my mother — a sweet face framed by dark braids and an ample bosom — but she was always warm, calm, patient and seemed to think I was special. She had me to lunch at her house one time and my elation was tempered only by the fear of doing something wrong. When it was decided to return me to regular school (either my place was needed for somebody punier or my mother thought I wasn't getting enough stimulation) there was some worry about my not being far enough ahead in math to keep up with the regular fifth grade. (We spent so much time resting and snacking that we didn't progress as fast.) Mrs. Evans stayed after school just for me and taught me division of fractions in less than an hour. Fortunately, I got plenty of practice on them when I returned to my old school and the dreaded drill mistress, Miss Tartongue, but I sure missed Mrs. Evans.

My worst school memory is also of Sunshine School. We were integrated into the regular Thousand Oaks School for recess and lunch and it was a large school of several hundred. The thirty or so Sunshiners were often teased by the other kids for being puny or different. There was a big cafeteria with many tables and we outsiders usually sat together for moral support. The food was supposed to be especially healthy, but I didn't like it much. One noon I wasn't feeling very well; my stomach hurt and I didn't want to eat at all. I poked at my macaroni and cheese and was urged to try the stewed rhubarb, which did not look very pretty. But it was too sweet, slimy and stringy and I had barely gotten it down before it came up again — all over my tray which fortunately was still in front of me. I was completely mortified and fled out onto the playground and into the girls' restroom. I refused to go back in the classroom when it was time and was escorted to the nurse's office to lie on a hard cot clutching an emesis basin until someone could come to take me home. I still felt disgraced when I returned to school and have never since been able to eat rhubarb in any form. I was glad to return to my neighborhood school, except for the sorrow of losing Mrs. Evans.

AWARENESS OF SEX

I knew nothing about sex when I was four years old and my mother found me rubbing my private parts when she came to tuck me in bed. After she talked to me so seriously about how I might hurt myself "down there" and how that part of me should be left alone and protected until I was grown up, I knew there was something special about that area of my body. It wasn't just for discovering pleasant sensations or for going to the toilet.

I had no brothers and had never seen my father naked; he was even embarrassed if I happened upon him in his long white union suit. But that year I got a new playmate, a four year old boy who moved in next door. Morton and I used to dress up and play we were getting married, then that we were parents to my family of dolls, though we had no idea how babies were made. I did become aware that Morton had different equipment "down there" and I admired and envied his ability to pee standing up. Once we had a contest, out on the sidewalk between our houses, in which I was allowed to use a six inch piece of garden hose because of my "handicap." Still, I was easily out-peed. We might have explored our differences further, but Morton moved away and I gave little more thought to male genitals until I reached adolescence.

My parents slept in separate beds which were placed on opposite sides of their large bedroom. On the morning of my sixth birthday, I found a longed-for stuffed Tigger on my bed when I woke up. I was so thrilled that I took my new toy into my parents' bedroom to thank them. They were both in my mother's twin bed, which seemed very odd to me, and though they made room for me to squeeze in between their nightclothes clad bodies, I had the feeling they were not entirely pleased to see me. Of course, I had no idea that frustrated sex was probably the cause of their discomfort.

By the time I got to high school, I must have known the scientific facts about how babies are made and have seen textbook drawings of male and female parts, but the act itself did not disturb the romantic fantasies I had about some of the handsome boys at school. Back then, before tight jeans became fashionable, there was little indication of sexual curiosities inside those baggy corduroy pants. I was late in reaching puberty, fourteen and a half and a junior in high school. I did have a good figure, loudly admired by the boys in my church youth group, and it was the minister's son, Arnold Westwood, who gave me my first kiss. His lips were soft and squishy and I didn't much enjoy it. I never had a real date in high school and the only sexual stimulation I got was from myself. (My mother's lecture could not prevail against teenage hormones.)

During my first year of college, I grew to love the romantic songs of Frank Sinatra, Tommy Dorsey, Glenn Miller and Benny Goodman, but they were about LOVE with only vague references to sex, as in the song "All of Me," which I found thrillingly insinuating. But I also began listening to songs by Duke Ellington, Billie Holliday, Ella Fitzgerald and some of the old Blues greats, which told of the darker side of love and had a sexier feel and more suggestive words.

I endured a few more unexciting kisses from occasional dates, but I was never turned on sexually until Ed (my future husband) and I fell in love and began to explore each other's bodies in what was known, first, as necking and then became "heavy petting." I was eighteen and ready, but we were both terrified of my getting pregnant. I learned what condoms were by reading a story in the college literary magazine (how shocking to see that word in print!), but I also learned they were a very unreliable means of protection. Besides, we had no safe, comfortable place to go. Borrowing my mother's Plymouth occasionally gave us a potentially more protected spot to make love than the hills above campus, but it was too awkward and unromantic a setting. And Ed, seven years older than I, had a noble old-fashioned notion that he should preserve my virginity. So we did everything we could think of short of going "all the way." In the first flush of our intimacy, I remember floating on air between my college classes; I knew I was still, technically, a virgin, but I thought I must look different to all around me. If the Army hadn't taken Ed away for many months, and if we hadn't decided to get married as soon as we could be reunited, I doubt I would have arrived at marriage still a virgin.

The Opposite Sex

I knew I was supposed to be interested in boys — they were what all the popular girls talked about — but I didn't really like boys when I was ten or eleven or twelve. I tried to keep up appearances, though. I went to a ballroom dancing class, at my mother's insistence, where the scrubbed and slicked down boys and the frilly, curly girls learned to do a sedate two-step around the upstairs hall over the drugstore where the Rotary met in the evenings. We all had to wear white gloves and learn polite protocol.

I was invited to a boy and girl party at which Spin the Bottle and Post Office were played. The boy who got me gave me a glancing peck somewhere near my mouth but I couldn't see what the other girls were shrieking and giggling about. I just wanted the party to be over.

My junior high had noontime dances in the multipurpose room and after observing a few times and practicing a little with my friend Elinor I felt brave enough to want to go to the Valentines Day Dance. You had to come with a partner, though, so I screwed up my courage and asked Alan Foster, the boy who sat by me in Latin and who was one of the few boys who spoke to me. Alan was barely as tall as I, a very quiet, self-effacing type but good at Latin, like me. I had him figured as easy to bully and when he said he couldn't dance I insisted that I could teach him quickly. He was still very reluctant so I offered him some candy and my 25 cent allowance if he would accompany me. He looked distressed but couldn't resist so we went and stumbled around the dance floor a few times. It wasn't much fun, but I was there doing what the other girls did.

When I was twelve, Gargo and I were invited to go on a driving trip to that still unfinished Boulder (now Hoover) Dam by our next door neighbor, the formidable Dr. Price. Accompanying us would be the boy who lived in Dr. Price's apartment house. His name was Robert and he was a couple of years older than I, dark haired and stocky. He practiced the trumpet, rather too loudly for neighborly comfort, but he was always pleasant when we met on the walk between our houses. Dr. Price had taken him on as a sort of god-grandson on whom he bestowed educational enrichment. It was Easter Vacation so school was no problem. We piled into Dr. Price's 1933 Buick with the old folks in front and the youngsters in back. If I had felt romantic about Robert it would have been a thrilling opportunity to get to know him, but mostly I just found it difficult to make conversation as we rode the long miles across the desert. I suppose he regarded me as a child, with my flat figure and kinky new perm (the first I'd ever had; I didn't know you were supposed to set it). Gargo and Dr. Price filled in most of the silences with lengthy discourses on California history, water politics, nature study and the like. The wildflowers were beautiful that spring, a discovery for me. Dr. Price drove like a madman; we stayed several nights at auto courts, en route to and in Boulder City, and got lots of information about the huge, impossible dam and life in the desert, very little of which I retained. Robert and I got along fine — like distant cousins. But a couple of years later, when I needed a date for some high school affair, I invited Robert as the only boy I knew, and he very politely agreed to come. It was a dull evening and I never went out with him again. Before long he left for college.

I did have a crush in junior high — on an older man, the

student teacher in my ninth grade English class. His name was Robert, also, but the girls in class called him Bobby because they thought he was cute. He was small in stature, fair-haired and pale, with a childish face and big blue eyes. His hands were delicate with long, tapering fingers that are said to indicate an artistic or romantic temperament, but he was a whiz at tennis. He wore a cheap pale blue suit and combed his hair neatly in class, but I had spotted him on the Cal tennis courts, all in white with his blond hair blowing in the breeze.

I got his attention by being a good student so I was able to persuade myself that he thought me special. I took to following him secretly after school or hanging out near where he lived and shopped on Telegraph Avenue. Then I could run into him as if by chance and be rewarded with his friendly smile and pretty blue eyes. But he finished his student teaching and I never saw him again.

My only really upsetting experience with the opposite sex in those days came from a completely unexpected — thus especially shocking — source. Gargo's old friends and our neighbors, Dr. and Mrs. Allen, invited Gargo and me to spend a few days with them at their cabin on the San Lorenzo River. Mrs. Allen was Gargo's birding and Cornell Women's Club crony and Dr. Allen was a respected professor emeritus of Greek at UC Berkeley. He was a large, fleshy old man, almost bald, with a beaky nose and glinting steel spectacles, but he could be jolly when he wanted to and liked to tease me gently. I was twelve and had just finished a sewing class at school in which I made myself a shorts outfit from delicate blue and green plaid cotton I had picked out myself. I was very proud of my accomplishment and eager to wear it in the world outside the classroom.

When we reached the cabin, after a long, sickeningly winding drive, we ladies went to freshen up before tea on the porch overlooking the river. I put on my new playsuit and went out

OVERCOMING CHILDHOOD ADVANTAGES

on the porch. Gargo and Mrs. Allen were still chatting but Dr. Allen was there, sitting on the swing glider. He smiled and invited me over so I sat beside him, and feeling the freedom and comfort of wearing shorts for the first time that summer, I bent my knees and put my feet up on the seat in front of me. We watched the slow flowing river through dappled sun and the smell of honeysuckle. Then I felt Dr. Allen's big hand sliding up the back of my exposed thigh inside the leg of my shorts and all the way to my panty line. I was horrified, jumped up and went in the house and tried to avoid the old man the rest of the time we were there.

When I told Gargo what happened, she said, "You shouldn't sit with your legs up like that," making it all my fault. Years later, I am still appalled that my supposedly feminist, progressive grandmother could have betrayed me like that. I was still a flat chested child and had never thought of myself as seductive. Fortunately, the experience didn't turn me off to men later on, just to dirty old men.

Love Notes

During the Depression, my family rented rooms in our big house to Cal instructors and others who were still getting salaries, however small. One of these roomers was Ann Landsburg, who wove original fabrics for some arty decorator in San Francisco. I guess the decorator wasn't doing much business because Ann worked most of the time as a secretary for one of the Chancellors. She was a striking looking young woman with long black hair usually twisted up in a coil on the back of her neck, and she wore exotic jewelry and colorful, flowing garments very unlike the sedate dress of my mother and grandmother.

I was 11 or 12, feeling lonely and left out, and Ann was very nice to me. She often invited me into her room, the big one that had been my grandmother's. (My grandmother now had my old room and my sister — who had also been ousted from her room — and I shared the top floor glassed in sun porch.) Ann would let me watch her working on her big loom, throwing the shuttle back and forth and creating beautiful cloth. Always, the record player would be playing beautiful, classical music. She had a man friend, Hans, who came often and stayed a long time and when he was there she didn't invite me in. Sometimes I would stand in the hall by her door and try to hear what they were saying or doing, but the music always blotted out whatever was going on.

Ann's attentions to me made me feel worthwhile and appreciated, and I began to want to be with her every day and to have feelings of longing I didn't understand. One day, as I stood outside her door listening to the soulful sounds of Cesar Franck's Symphony, I decided to write a note to Ann. I wrote, "I love you" on a slip of paper and slid it under her door. Then, appalled at what I had done, I ran out of the house and went walking in the hills.

I had learned, at least vaguely, what a lesbian was when I was nine and a couple of tenants of that persuasion were living in our smaller house next door. I already knew about men living together — there were quite a few of those in Berkeley — but that was the first I had heard about women loving each other like that. I knew such women were snickered about and called names, and now I was afraid I might be like that and felt ashamed.

I didn't go back home until suppertime and my family was already at the table. I was scolded for being gone so long without letting anyone know where I was, but nothing was said about my note until after supper. Then my mother, the budding psychologist, took me aside and said that Ann had shown her my note but that it was OK at my age to have feelings like that. I would get over them. But she told me to stop bothering Ann so much, and I knew my wonderful visits to her room would not last.

Ann was still kind to me and she never mentioned the note, but she spent more and more time with Hans. When she moved out to get married it hardly hurt me at all. By then I had a crush on Robert, my student teacher in English. When I took up weaving, years later, I didn't connect it with my admiration for Ann and her work. But whenever I hear the Cesar Franck D Minor Symphony I remember that time and the feelings I had then.

People Don't Like You For Your I.Q.

That's what Gargo said but I had the notion that my mother felt differently. After she acquired a four year old stepdaughter and especially after my arrival two years later, my mother's main interest switched from botany to child development and psychology. She returned to U.C., working as a student intern and then as an associate for the Institute of Child Development there.

Lewis Terman's long-term study of gifted children was a big thing then and, though my sister was not included in it, a number of her friends were. Terman developed the Stanford-Binet Intelligent Test — which popularized the term I.Q. (for Intelligence Quotient) — a number arrived at by dividing a child's score or "Mental Age" by his/her chronological age. Thus, a six year old with a Mental Age of nine years would have an I.Q. of 150. The sub tests were arranged in order of age difficulty, with the questions for each age level supposedly answerable by a child of average intelligence for that age. You could miss some questions at your age level and still score average if you passed some at a higher age level.

For her college work, my mother needed subjects to practice and demonstrate on and, of course, my sister and I were her first choices. I think my sister got off the hook by the time I was four, maybe because by then she was at school in Switzerland, so from then on I was the main guinea pig. I know I was used to demonstrate the test both at the Institute (in a room with one-way mirrors) and before a larger audience. My memory is of being up on a stage in a huge auditorium but that can't be true — only metaphorical. Some of the tests were fun — arranging colored blocks to copy increasingly difficult patterns, drawing my way out of mazes or matching pictures that had similarities in some way not immediately obvious. Many of the verbal tests were fun, too, until they got too hard. The test required that the examiner keep going until the subject had missed all questions for at least one age level so I always ended with a feeling of failure, to my mother especially.

One time I tried to cheat. I believe I was about six and Mother was testing me in our dining room. We got to a question in which I was supposed to say what time it would be if the hands on the clock were reversed, e.g. 9:25 would be 5:45. I simply couldn't do it in my head, but I knew I could if I got hold of a clock. I asked my mother if she would like me to get her slippers for her. No. Was she cold didn't she want her sweater? No, she was fine. Well, I had to go to the bathroom. Then she let me go and didn't accompany me. I went upstairs, found the alarm clock, turned the hands to the appropriate position, flushed the toilet and went back downstairs to give the answer. My mother never asked me why I didn't use the downstairs bathroom but she didn't ask me any more clock questions either and soon the test was over.

All that testing must have influenced my decision, after I had children of my own, to switch my field from biology to school psychology and psychometry. Certainly, I was following my mother's pattern. I don't think I was getting revenge; I didn't enjoy making kids squirm when they didn't know the answers. By the time I was testing children, the Stanford-Binet teat was rarely used except for bright children. It was known to give an advantage to verbally fluent, culturally enriched kids. For the others, we used performance or non-language tests along with many other types of evaluation. And I had long since learned that people don't like you for your I,Q.

Teen age fooling around.

My sister as a faculty wife.

Junior High Daze

I started Claremont Junior High School in Oakland when I was ten years old. My hair was worn in the straight Dutch-boy cut that my father said made me look like a Norman prince (Oh, boy!). My clothes were usually something baggy, hand knit by my grandmother, Gargo, or little girl dresses with Peter Pan collars, puffed sleeves and ties at the waist. (My figure was almost two dimensional so it didn't matter a lot what I wore.) Neither my mother nor my grandmother wore lipstick or approved of it, though I suspect my sixteen year old sister put it on as soon as she left the house. My shoes were sensible, clumpy brown oxfords. I knew I was supposed to be interested in boys — they were what all the popular girls talked about but I regarded them as being either loud, dirty and uncouth or inept babyish sissies. I met with my first classroom difficulties in seventh grade. My favorite class was Latin. I found the cadences of *Hic, haec, hoc, Gallia est omnis divisa* and *Arma virumque cano* exciting and easy for me. Many in the class were having troubles, though, and the teacher had to go over things so many times that I would get bored. My nerdy friend, Alan Foster, was also having an easy time with the language, so while the teacher was helping those who were struggling, Alan and I would do our assignment and start whispering or passing notes to each other. Occasionally, we shot a spit wad or two, but it wasn't long before the teacher caught us at that and gave us a severe lecture. When report cards came out, at the end of the first quarter, I got an "A" in Latin for subject matter but a "C" in Citizenship! I was stunned and my mother and grandmother were horrified. I had always been such a good little girl. Since my mother was working, it was up to my grandmother to come to school and deal with this disgraceful situation. I was mortified to have my Gargo, with her old-fashioned shoes and hats and her sensible (dowdy) clothes walking with me down the hall to the principal's office. I don't remember exactly what was said in that solemn meeting but after that I didn't pass any more notes or shoot any more spit wads. I think I took to doodling but I loved Latin enough to keep on with it through the tenth grade.

My next favorite class was English, which was also easy for me, but mostly because of our beautiful young teacher named Delight Phillips. She had shiny, black hair which she piled up on her head in various intricate arrangements, puffy, bright pink lips which always glistened and fashionable clothes of a cut and color to show off her admirable figure. She was very different from any of my elementary school teachers. Since she was single, there was much speculation among the girls about her love life. (I don't know what the boys were saying but I can imagine.) By late in the first semester, she was often seen in the halls at lunch time talking intensely and intimately with the Boys' P.E. teacher, whom I regarded as an empty headed hunk. I felt betrayed that someone so lovely and so dedicated to fine literature could be attracted to such a macho lamebrain. Nevertheless, they were married the next summer and Delight left teaching, at least at Claremont.

I thought I would like my Art class because I had always enjoyed fooling around with art and craft projects but it turned out to be a disaster. This was formal instruction in color and design but mostly in copying still lifes. My rendition of a plate of fruit was so far from what the teacher wanted that she gave me a "C" in the class, the first "C" I ever got in a subject. My father pronounced the teacher a discredit to her profession but I was so upset that I didn't take another Art class until I was in my fifties.

Math wasn't much fun, either. It was all about compound interest and the stock market and other stuff that didn't seem to have anything to do with me. But we did learn how to make out money orders, bank checks and deposit and withdrawal slips which seemed pretty grown up and useful.

Social Studies was a little more interesting. The Okies were coming to California., Roosevelt was making big changes in the country and Civil War was brewing in Spain. I had a problem, though, when we were assigned to listen to the Richfield Reporter at 10:00 P.M. because my bedtime was still at 8:00. I finally was able to get a note from the teacher to my parents asking for a special dispensation so I could fulfill my assignment. It was a humiliating request.

I had been introduced to nonacademic classes like Woodshop and Chorus in elementary school but now I got to learn about Cooking and Sewing, which I had not been taught at home, except to help Gargo with treats like fudge or gingerbread. In Sewing, I found that I didn't enjoy the process as much as the product, especially if I were making something I wanted to wear. There were no boys in the class and our first project was a dainty, white batiste slip, a garment I never expected to wear. There was lace trim around the bosom (what bosom!) and lots of hand finishing and the teacher, a wrinkled, tight lipped old woman who always wore the same dark, tailored suit, would walk up and down the aisles, examining our needlework and often proclaiming "Rip it out! Rip it out!" so we would try again more painstakingly. I hated her. But it was fun to learn to use the electric sewing machine even though that kind of stitching was very hard to rip out.

My grandmother still used her old treadle Singer which sewed easy-to-rip chainstitch and on which she could sew almost as fast as the electrics. She had helped me make a few things like doll blankets and pot holders but I had a hard time coordinating feet and hands.

Our second sewing project was a one-piece cotton playsuit with a button-front skirt of the same material, something I knew I would enjoy wearing. I picked out some pretty fine-line green-and-blue plaid and after several false starts (I think I sewed the shorts legs to each other), numerous rippings and an agony of sore fingers over the buttonholes, I produced an outfit I was proud to wear. What a triumph! I even retained enough of what I learned to make shirts and dresses for myself and my family years later.

Cooking was less stressful and I enjoyed eating most of the things we made in that class. When the students picked partners, Leonard Cohen — the only boy in the class — and myself were the leftovers so we became partners by default. I had known Leonard for several years as he rode to school on the same streetcar I did and often teased and pestered me. I was not thrilled to have him as a partner but it turned out that he behaved himself in class and we got along as a pretty good team. He was more daring, but I cleaned up better. We got to eat everything we made, after setting the table in the approved manner, removing our aprons and washing our hands. I couldn't eat the Brussel sprouts au gratin but I loved a thick malt milk shake, full of nutritious supplements and supposed to be good for invalids. I often made it after the class was over, whether of not anyone in my family was sick. But by the time I got married, I had lost that recipe and had to learn to cook all over again.

Gym class was a time of acute discomfort for me. We girls had to wear white gym suits and our changing room was a big

OVERCOMING CHILDHOOD ADVANTAGES

barn-like portable with lockers and benches around the sides. There was not the slightest opportunity for privacy. While the other girls were comparing their new bras, I was attempting to hide my flat chested undershirt as quickly as possible under my gym top. Some girls got excused from playing because they were having their "period." They called it "The Curse." While I knew this referred to menstruation I was still unclear about the details of the process. Did the bleeding come from blood that would have gone into a baby?

I was too uncoordinated to be any good at sports and was always among the last chosen for a team. Softball was what I dreaded most. I couldn't hit the ball and I kept spraining my fingers when trying to catch. One girl called me "Unco". The gym teacher was kind, though, and tried to encourage me. Once, when I had been out sick, she let me be scorekeeper. I stood on the sidelines, daydreaming more than watching, and completely forgot to count the runs. At the end, when I was asked the final score, I panicked and ad-libbed "Three to six", not even saying which team scored which. The girls all groaned and gave me disgusted looks and the teacher gave me a long, disappointed look but she walked with me back to the locker room and helped me save face by warding off the girls' demands for an explanation.

My one moment of glory at softball was aborted by a spectacular accident. I had actually hit the ball far enough (or the fielders were clumsy enough) that I seemed sure of making a home run. I was just rounding third base when the baseman stuck out her foot (I'm sure of it!). I tripped and fell hard, landing on the point of my chin on the blacktop. Immediately bright blood gushed out and soaked the front of my white gym suit and I had the attention of everyone on the field. The teacher and several girls helped me inside, cleaned me up, bandaged my chin, called my mother at work and waited with me until she arrived to take me for stitches. When I returned to school the next day, I found myself getting more awed and solicitous attention — but of course, that didn't last as long as it took to get the stitches out.

Those first two years in Junior High, I was pretty much of an oddball and largely ignored by my classmates. My only friends were a couple of other lost souls — Elinor and Barbara. Elinor was blond, pretty in a pie-faced way, poor and motherless. She lived with her father in a series of dismal basement apartments — the kind of housing I hadn't known existed. Her father was a cook who kept having to find another job or another living space because he had a drinking problem. My mother didn't really approve of my friendship with Elinor; she would have been even more disturbed if she had seen inside some of the grungy places where Elinor took me home to visit — cold, empty, disorderly and ugly. But for me it was an adventure to see how differently other people lived.

Barbara had all the right credentials — a professor for a father, a gracious mother who was always there when Barbara took me to her clean, tastefully decorated home overlooking the Bay — but Barbara was unattractive and even more socially inept than I. Tall and gawky, with dental braces, a large bony nose and stringy, dark hair, she wore the kind of dresses and shoes I did and always looked as if she were only partially assembled. I think Elinor and I were her only friends and we turned out to be rotten ones. Barbara's twelfth birthday was coming up and Elinor and I decided to get her a "joke" present. We went to the nearby dime store at lunch hour and, with our pooled allowances, we got a bar of Lifebuoy soap, a small bottle of Listerine, some deodorant, and a pair of old lady garters to improve our friend's personal grooming. We put the collection in an empty candy box and wrapped it prettily, then presented it to our victim. I can still see Barbara's look of happy expectation changing to one of puzzlement and hurt as she examined the contents while we explained what each item would do for her. We tried, halfheartedly, to pass it off as a joke but by then I didn't think it was very funny either. The saddest part was that Barbara needed our companionship so badly that she didn't even get mad at us — just very quiet.

By the time I was twelve and in the ninth grade I didn't see Elinor or Barbara much anymore. I was learning to look and act like the girls I admired and to hang around in their aura, even though I still wasn't much interested in boys. I tried to keep up appearances, though.

My father thought I looked much more "handsome" with straight hair and wearing what are now called "earth tones". But I think my mother understood; she, too, was trying to break out of the Ivory Tower and live like a modern woman of the 1930s. My sister was the biggest help. She came back from highschool in Germany in 1933, wearing a dirndl with a peplum, a loden-cloth cape and her hair in a bun, and entered public school for the first time. It was not long before she was wearing saddle shoes, sweaters and skirts, lipstick and a curly blond bob. During the next four years, until she left for graeduate school, she taught me how to lie convincingly to our strict guardians about where we were going, whom we were going with and what we would be doing while gone; how to talk on the telephone, how to act with boys and even how to laugh at our troubles.

Rosalie, 10. Helena, 16.

Helena, 19. Rosalie, 13..

OVERCOMING CHILDHOOD ADVANTAGES

Three misfits: me, age 10 $^1/_2$, Elinor, and Barbara. 7th Grade, 1934.

Jean, Betty, Me. Age 16.

Summer Romance

When I graduated from high school in the summer of '39, I was not quite sixteen and had never had a date. Since my mother worked, my grandmother was in charge of my vacation time. I had gone to summer school for six weeks in order to finish up some requirements for entering Cal in August, but I had a few weeks of free time in between, so my grandmother, whom my family called Gargo, arranged to take me to Fallen Leaf Lake for two weeks, a favorite vacation haunt for us. In those days, the housekeeping camp at the lake was owned by some Stanford alumni and was primarily for the enjoyment of families from that college. Gargo happened to know the owners, though she had gone to Cornell, not Stanford, and she rented us a nice tent-cabin for our stay there. I was very excited, for I loved Fallen Leaf and I felt I was poised at a big stepping stone in my life and that something wonderful would happen there to mark the beginning of my new freer and more grown-up existence. I was very interested in boys but the ones I admired — the handsome, smart, sought after ones — did not even know I existed and those who were interested in me were the kind who would now be termed "nerds" and I avoided them.

I had learned a little about dancing and flirting by going to the Unitarian youth group and I had even allowed the minister's son to kiss me once, for the experience, even though I thought he was a jerk. Packing to go to Fallen Leaf, I indulged in all sorts of romantic fantasies. I got a new bathing suit to show off my figure (which even the Unitarian boys whistled at), new shorts, a floaty beach robe to wear down to the boat dock, a new perm and lipstick. Then I planned how I could make our tent-cabin a more attractive place to entertain young male visitors. I must have imagined Gargo would disappear on a walk or to an evening campfire, leaving me alone with my willing prey. I packed a fragrant pillow which bore the message "I Pine for You and Balsam, Too." I put in some candles and small pewter candlesticks, an embroidered linen table runner and a flowered bureau scarf. The book I had read most recently was *Gone With the Wind,* but I didn't think that would impress a prospective boy friend. I hadn't gotten into Emily Dickinson yet so I decided I wasn't qualified to discuss literature but I did take along my worn and beloved stuffed Tigger and Eeyore as symbols of my sensitive upbringing. Gargo was puzzled by my extra baggage but allowed me to bring whatever I could carry. Since Gargo didn't drive, my mother delivered us to the lake one weekend and would come pick us up in two weeks. Our tent-cabin was standard: two steel cots with Army blankets, a bureau, a rack for hangers, a small table and chairs, a wood stove and one overhead electric light bulb hanging down from the ridgepole. I did my best, with what I had brought, to turn it into an inviting spider's parlor but I had to admit it needed a great deal more than I could provide. Some pine cones and sprigs of evergreen helped but I decided the wooden deck outside, where the picnic table and benches were, along with a couple of classic but uncomfortable Adirondack chairs, was a more promising spot to entertain my first conquest.

 The sun filtered through the tall pines, the chipmunks and ground squirrels dashed and chased each other in and out of the woodpile and the air smelled wonderful. Gargo went in to take her nap and I put on my bathing suit and headed for the boat dock, where I knew the action was. It wasn't long before I was able to attach myself to two girls about my age, Joan and Betty, who were sunning themselves and watching the scene. They, too were going to be college freshmen but I was careful not to reveal my tender age, only my educational level. The dock was where all the rental boats were tied up as well as where the private boats from the summer homes around the lake came in to moor while their owners went to the small grocery store and snack bar at the resort. The private boat drivers were envied and denigrated by us tent-cabin renters. They stayed in expensive vacation homes, wore snooty yachting caps and had high-powered boats which they liked to roar away from the dock, leaving us all rocking and awash. They were said to have noisy, drunken parties. Jean and Betty and I didn't think we had a chance with any of these rich kids but the boys who handled the rental boats all Stanford students, as were the other camp employees were fair game. They knew everything about the boats and how to handle them, either with oars or outboards, and leapt in and out of them with supreme nonchalance, across what seemed like remarkable spans of water. The one I fastened on was named John; he was very tan and muscular and the hair on his head, chest and limbs was bleached blond by a summer in the sun. He would be a junior at Stanford. In between rental customers, the boat boys had time to chat with children and old ladies and to kid around with pretty young girls. Within a few days we had a triple date arranged to go to the Tahoe casinos for an evening; one of the boys had an old Hudson with a rumble seat so we could all squeeze in. I told Gargo we were going to a movie in South Tahoe and brought John up to the cabin to meet her but he never got to see my interior decorating. I remember very little about that evening. I don't think any of us had a drink — even the boys weren't twenty-one yet — and we must have just drifted around the casinos and watched the goings-on. Coming back to camp, huddled together in the rumble seat to keep warm, John kissed me. The softness and warmth of his lips felt strangely pleasant but no rockets went off for me. Still, I was determined to learn more about boy-girl relations before I started college, so when John asked me to go out with him alone the next night, I accepted. He didn't have a car so we rented a rowboat and went out on the lake. (I have no idea what I told my grandmother I was doing, but she was an innocent sort. My mother would have been much more suspicious.) We glided out onto the black lake, watching the lights on shore grow more distant and the stars overhead grow more brilliant and numerous. John had brought pillows and a blanket and when he found a quiet place to anchor we cuddled in the bottom of the boat and gazed skyward. It was not a very comfortable arrangement and I had no idea what I was supposed to do or say. John's hands were exploring my well protected breasts, through several layers of clothes and a containing bra, but what I felt was mostly cramped and increasingly chilly. We rowed around some more. It really was lovely out there under the stars but we got too cold and finally headed back to the snack bar for hot cocoa.

The rest of my stay there I think John and I spent walking and talking, with some hand holding and a few kisses. John felt Stanford was superior to Cal, of course, and made me feel defensive about going there. He was twenty and, though I'm not sure I ever told him I was only sixteen, I felt he patronized me. We parted with promises that he would come visit me in Berkeley as soon as he could, but somehow I didn't feel thrilled at that prospect. just felt we should see each other again. He did come to Berkeley, early in the semester. The World's Fair was happening on Treasure Island and he invited me to spend the day there with him. I felt awkward as soon as he arrived at my front door. I had overdressed in going-to-the-city garb which looked school girlish beside his casual collegiate elegance, and I didn't know what to talk about. I had joined a sorority and he made fun of me for that because it was not one of the Top Ten. We talked about our classes and instructors and, once the train delivered us to the Fair, about the exhibits and the rides but it all felt like an effort. Without the sparkling lake, the vaulting mountains and the scent of pine, we had very little in common. The roller coaster ride upset my stomach and by evening I was more than ready to go home. When John delivered me back to my house, he spoke vaguely about the next time he came to Berkeley, but I never saw or heard from him again. Strangely, I felt more relief than hurt. I had taken my first baby steps into a new world and survived.

Carmel Beach, 1939.

CAL

I was just a few weeks past my sixteenth birthday when I enrolled as one of 4000 freshmen at U.C. Berkeley in 1939.

It was mid August, still warm, lazy summer days, but I was thrilled to be starting college, even though I had spent most of my vacation going to summer school. I bathed and dressed carefully for this rite of passage: pleated, plaid skirt, too hot blue angora sweater with matching socks and, of course, Roos Brothers brown and white saddle shoes. I fluffed out my pin curls, dabbed makeup on my red blotches of acne and marched the six blocks down the hill from my home to the campus, feeling as I imagined I would feel at a long anticipated debut or religious ceremony.

Joining the growing line of new students on Bancroft Way below Telegraph, I proceeded, a few steps at a time, along Dana Street and into the new Men's Gym for registration. I'd been in the Gym before for basketball games and concerts but now it was transformed into a maze of roped off lines, waiting areas, writing areas, alphabetical categories, residence categories, declared majors, undeclared majors, with restrictive signs at every turn and stern faced (or bored) monitors to enforce them. I had declared my major as "PreMed" — my mother's idea, since I supposedly had the same scientific bent she did — and finally I found an appropriate "advisor", one of the many perched uncomfortably at card tables in the central bull pen. He signed my program: Zoology 1A, Chemistry 1A, English 1A, World

History and German 3, and advised me to put "NMI" instead of the "X" I had written in confused response to the demand for a middle initial. (Could there really be more than one Rosalie Steilberg?) I paid my $16 fee and became a brand new member of the Class of '43.

The next days were exciting — and painful. I was going through sorority rushing — also my mother's idea because I needed to become more social. I hated the dressing up in stockings, heels, a girdle, hat and gloves — clothes I never wore and was not comfortable in. I felt insecure in the tottery heels, worried about my stocking seams being straight, my slip showing, my hat at the wrong angle. But mostly I had no idea what to talk about; I knew I was being rushed only because of my high grades in high school and my potential ability for raising a sorority's overall GPA. None of the Big Ten houses invited me for more than an initial courtesy tea but the sorority my mother had belonged to invited me back several times, I suspected because I was what is known as a "legacy". Then came the last night and the issuing of bids: I received only one bid, and it was not from my mother's sorority. I was crushed: there must be something really wrong with me, a legacy, to have been blackballed. I wasn't much interested in the sorority which did send me a bid but my mother urged me to accept it, for my social development, and with utter lack of enthusiasm, I did.

My first classes, though, I found both thrilling and strange. My high school graduating class numbered about 400 students; now I found myself packed into lecture halls holding 500. The professors were performers and most of them put on a fascinating show. Joel Hildebrand in Chemistry was especially good at complicated Goldbergian constructions and tricks to illustrate his points. The History professor had less to work with and the poor ventilation in Wheeler Hall, plus the one o'clock hour, sometimes caused me to doze and drop my pen.

It would go rolling noisily down the aisle, much to my embarrassment. There, were plenty of slides and other visual aids in Zoology to keep me interested but the really exciting classes were the small sections and labs. I was assigned a worktable, a locker and a partner in both Chemistry and Zoology labs and a microscope as well for the latter. Squinting through the scope with my (I later learned) astigmatic left eye, I discovered and managed to draw (I who had drawn nothing since seventh grade!) a reasonable likeness of a paramecium, a flagellate, a hydra. Later, I progressed to dissecting and drawing a worm, a frog, a shark. What marvels! I developed a crush on my lab instructor, a kind, helpful young man in a white coat that never seemed to get dirty.

I bought a white lab coat, too, which I believed flattered my figure and which protected my sweaters and skirts from the corrosive effects of the various liquids I was mixing up in Chemistry lab. My fingers, however, and especially my right thumb, with which I stoppered test tubes while shaking them, turned rough and yellow, as if I had been smoking heavily for years. My science classes had the added interest of consisting mostly of boys, with the few other girls being, in my opinion, not very attractive ones. I was not above using my charms to get boys to help me with solutions to problems, but too often I found that I knew more than they did — and they did not appreciate me for that.

My third year German class was small, of course, and had some upper classmen in it; we were reading Schiller and I thought that was pretty impressive. (Of course, we never spoke the language in those days.) English Composition, which I had expected to enjoy because I had found it easy in high school, was the source of my first comeuppance with University standards. Our T.A. was an intense young woman, quite dedicated to the English language and to its clear and graceful expression.

OVERCOMING CHILDHOOD ADVANTAGES

For our first essay assignment, I was feeling pressured for time by all the hours I was having to spend in labs and I decided to hand in, with a few alterations, a piece on Socialized Medicine on which I had received an A in Senior English just a few months earlier. I was appalled when Miss Dedicated Intensity returned it to me with a grade of C! I had not received such a shameful grade since seventh grade Art class, when I couldn't copy a still life properly. The notes which the T.A. wrote in the margins said things like "Insufficient Development" and "Sophomoric." (I was puzzled by the latter because, after all, I was only a freshman, so I had to look it up.)

My social life at the sorority was a masquerade: I went there for lunch several times a week and dinner on Monday nights when we had our meetings. I learned to dress, act and talk like a sorority girl, to sing the songs and take part in the ridiculous secret rituals (more maudlin than Camp Fire Girls, even) but I never learned to play bridge or gossip about boys. When asked to make up a foursome after lunch or dinner, I always begged off by saying I had a lab to get to or studying to do. A blind date was arranged for me for the Autumn dance but, though I enjoyed dressing up in a formal and thought I looked fine, the boy turned out to be a pleasant, polite dud and I never saw him again.

In October, at my now married sister's urging, I decided to join the University Chorus, which my professor brother-in-law now directed. It was already dark before seven o'clock but there was a harvest moon, rustling drifts of fallen leaves and the sharp smell of their burning as I walked across the windy campus to the Chorus meeting place. I had sung in my church choir and knew how to read music but I would have been too scared to audition and fortunately that wasn't required. I joined the Alto section, waved to my brother-in-law up at the front of the room and was immediately drawn to the person he was talking to — a tall, handsome, redheaded man who was a little older than most of the students. This man, I learned was known as the First Chorister and he was the Director's main assistant, music librarian, roll taker and organizer. He had a marvelous laugh that made everyone feel good and a beautiful bass voice, as I learned when we began practicing the music. We were learning the Mozart Requiem and it was the most thrilling music I had ever sung — nothing like the bland, smarmy hymns at church.

After that night, Chorus, became my favorite class and the First Chorister my primary love interest. I was interested in my other classes and was able to get good grades in most of them by studying hard, but there were a few subjects that stumped me. The first of these was a Chemistry class in Quantitative Analysis. For all my careful measuring and mixing, I couldn't seem to come up with the right quantities to fit the equations and at the first midterm period I received a grade of D. I was so appalled that I dropped the course and tried again during summer session when I could concentrate on just that subject and get a lot of help and encouragement from Bill, the tall, nerdy Teaching Assistant. I worked many hours in the lab, went out with Bill a couple of times (Dullsville!) and got a "B" in the course.

My next stumbling block was Embryology and the lab that went with it: Microtechnique. Both classes were taught by Dr. Joseph Abraham Long, a sour curmudgeon who was the terror of the Zoology Department. His explanations of the various stages of developing embryos in chicks and humans never did come clear for me and I had to be satisfied with a "C" my second such grade at Cal, the first having been in Econ 1A which I never understood, either. Microtechnique lab was worse. We had to make slides of tissue samples which we prepared ourselves in a long, tricky, complicated process. The hardest part for me was slicing the tissue block (about the size of a sugar cube) with the microtome, just thin enough to see through without making it so thin it ruptured, then staining, it — not too dark and not too light. I had to start the whole process over many times and must have spent at least six hours a week on what was supposed to be a three hour lab, trying to get my slides to satisfy the terrifying Dr. Long. I never succeeded and got a "D" in the class, the shame of my college career but fortunately only one unit worth.

My final downfall was in Physics. Again, it was the lab course that was so baffling to me. In the biological sciences and even in Chemistry, there were tangible and/or observable substances and entities which I could manipulate or draw and something to understand. In Physics, I was asked to believe in a multitude, of invisible waves or particles or forces zipping around and producing energy and actions which I seemed unable to recreate under lab conditions. In the lectures, I could memorize and regurgitate material I did not understand well enough to get a "B", but in the lab section I was supposed to prove principles which eluded me; I was lucky to get a "C".

There was one course I really loved and that was Physiology. The young instructor, a handsome Latino with a mop of black curls, had received departmental permission to conduct a small section for the top students in the class. About a dozen of us were selected, by grades and test scores I suppose, from the class of about 75. This elite group was run more like a seminar and I was tremendously stimulated to be working with a bunch of really bright, enthusiastic students in such a fascinating subject. We got to measure our own lung capacity, then ran up and down the stairs of the Life Sciences Building and measured it again. We got a large turtle to dissect to study the circulatory system. I'll never forget the sound of the tin snips crunching through the lower carapace! I'd done some dissecting in Anatomy class but now I was learning how all these organ systems worked. Every class meeting was a challenge and the final exam was an oral, in front of three professors — terrifying, but we all passed.

I was so totally immersed in my pursuits of love and learning that I paid very little attention to the war going on in Europe and Asia. I had listened to Hitler's rantings on the radio and knew him to be power-mad and evil but I never thought of him as a threat to my way of life. I knew that England was being bombed, that countries were being invaded, that everyone was upset with Chamberlain but none of that seemed to have much to do with me. The most immediate effect on my life, in the summer of '39, was that the graduation trip abroad that my grandmother had promised me had to be postponed indefinitely. I didn't even know any boys who got drafted, so Pearl Harbor came as a complete shock to me. I was a Junior, living in the sorority house that semester — a part of my mother's socialization program and, for me, a good chance to get away from home, even if it was only across the street. Ed, my First Chorister, and I were by now much in love. He was due to graduate in January and was worried about his likelihood of being drafted.

That Sunday morning, December 7, 1941, I was in my room at the sorority house, studying for finals. The news on the radio seemed unbelievable; some girls were frightened or in tears but I felt stunned and numb. None of us had any idea what it would mean but, looking out across San Francisco Bay, I knew we were living in a very vulnerable spot. Soon we had designated a "bomb shelter" in the furnace room of the sorority and were putting up blackout curtains on all the windows. Before long, the Japanese students and teachers began disappearing from our classes and from my parents' rented rooms. My mother went to work for the Red Cross, using her social work skills to help relocate Japanese families. We grew used to the sounds of blackout sirens, learned to find our way around in the dark and discovered nooks where we could study without any light showing. We grumbled about rationing but experienced no hardships from having less gas, or meat, or butter. We learned to apply liquid stockings, even to drawing a seam up the backs of our legs, but never discovered how to keep the tan makeup from rubbing off on our sheets at night. We rolled bandages for the Red Cross and learned to knit socks in olive drab wool. (The pair I made for Ed hurt his feet and he never wore them.) My family saved fat in old soup cans and aluminum foil in balls and dug up part of the front lawn for a Victory Garden, which I sometimes helped tend.

Squadrons of Naval cadets invaded the campus and some of the college boys disappeared into the Armed Services. A few of my sorority sisters married in desperate haste before their loved ones left. Once or twice I heard of a boy I had known slightly being killed overseas and that made me feel very sad and fearful. Ed was cynical about the war and about the part that heads of state and the military industrial powers had had in bringing it about. If fleeing to Canada or declaring himself a Conscientious Objector had been a real possibility in those days, I believe he would have done one or the other. But he was drafted in February, 1942 on his 26th birthday and sent to Fort Ord to be in the, Medical Corps, running blood tests on GI's and WAAC'S. I missed him terribly but knew how lucky we were to be so close geographically. He came up whenever he got a weekend pass and I visited him a couple of times at Fort Ord. I thought he looked very handsome in his Army khakis but I wished they hadn't cut his beautiful red hair so short

By the summer of '42, I had finished my three year pre-med course but knew I didn't want to be a doctor. I applied to only one medical school, U.C. San Francisco but it was just a gesture and the Admissions Committee, though impressed by my grades and test scores, was not impressed by my age (still eighteen), my sex and my lack of enthusiasm. To my relief, I didn't get in; I wanted to marry Ed as soon as possible, not be tied up in Medical School.

 Still, I felt I needed to do something for the War Effort. My father had just gone off to Kodiak, Alaska to build things for the Navy and my mother was a 'Psychiatric Social Worker' working with returned veterans at the Oakland Naval Hospital. I decided I should go to Nursing School at U.C.S.F. and by making up a couple of requirements during Intersession, was able to enroll for the summer term. Two friends of mine were caught up in the same patriotic fervor and we spent the summer months sharing a room in the nurses' dorm on Pill Hill. We explored the neighborhoods around that part of the City, walked in Golden Gate Park in the evenings (it was reasonably safe then), dated medical students, got top grades in all our classes, and experienced the realities of nursing care: bed pans, trays, bed baths, enemas and corpses and the humiliation of being treated like morons and slaves by the M.D.'s. Ed had told me I wouldn't like Nursing School and my parents had expressed grave doubts about my decision. All of them were right and we three star students all quit at the end of the semester, in spite of tremendous pressure to stay from the Director of Nurses and her staff.

 So now I had one year of college to get through before I could graduate and I needed a Major. With all those units in science courses, the easiest major for me turned out to be Zoology, and so I returned to Berkeley and signed up for the appropriate classes. Ed was shipped off to officer Candidate School in North Dakota, just in time to save him from being sent overseas on a hospital ship that was fated to be bombed to bits in the South Pacific. He and I had an "understanding" that we would marry someday but there was no formal engagement and I decided I needed to broaden my social life a little. So I dated occasionally, and halfheartedly, with the few 4F's and others still left on Campus. There was Wade, a pale, unimpressive strawberry blond, heir to the Daisy canopener fortune, who had a punctured ear drum or some such excuse and hinted at a life of ease for me. There was Armando, a Latin American studying Chemical Engineering who was planning to return to Uruguay (or wherever) and help to modernize his country's agriculture. I think he was offering me something but his accent was so heavy and his vocabulary so limited that I wasn't sure what it was. And there was Bill, the Chemistry T.A., with poor vision, sweaty hands and bad breath, who didn't promise me anything but did give me a "B".

Suddenly, it was May, 1943, I was about to graduate and had no notion what to do next. My sorority sisters were either getting married or finding dull sounding jobs with local businesses like Cutter's, KalKan or United Air Lines. I was tired of going to school and didn't want a higher degree, my parents' goal for me. I wanted to be with Ed. He had completed O.C.S. and was stationed at Fort Lewis, Washington. I wrote him a passionate letter and received, in return, a proposal and an engagement ring, which I wore proudly to my commencement ceremonies. We were married two months later, on my twentieth birthday, and I left Cal behind — though not forever. The marriage lasted 46 years, Ed's lifetime, and my love of choral music and fascination with living things still persist. Is a college education wasted on girls, as many people claim?

Lying for Love

I was eighteen, a Junior in college, and seriously in love for the first time. Ed and I had been going together for six months when he was drafted, soon after Pearl Harbor. But by a miracle of Army wisdom and compassion, he was stationed at Ford Ord, just a few hours away, and assigned to the Medical Corps. He got one two-day leave that spring and came to see me at my home in Berkeley but we missed each other terribly and our letters grew more and more desperate and overheated.

Finally Ed wrote asking me to visit him at the Fort. I could stay in the visitors' guest house and see him in the evenings and his free time since he worked regular hours as a lab technician. I knew my parents would never allow me to make such a trip alone so I determined to do it secretly. One of my sorority sisters, Lynn, lived near Salinas and I made up a story that she had invited me to spend the weekend with her at her parents' ranch. Lynn had her own car and would drive me down and back.

My grandmother was away somewhere and my parents were so busy working that they weren't even home when I packed my bag on Friday afternoon and carried it down the hill to catch the red F train for San Francisco. There, I walked over to Third and Townsend and boarded the Del Monte Express to Monterey. The conductor told me the train would slow down and stop briefly at Fort Ord so I could hop off. I had my Anatomy text and notes with me as we were having a midterm on Monday and I had to know the names, locations and functions of dozens of muscles, I tried to study on the train but it was hard to concentrate. The car was filled mostly with weekenders and their kids, headed for Carmel and Pacific Grove on the "Sunshine Special."

As we approached Fort Ord through the low sand hills reddened by frostnipped iceplant, I gave up memorizing and got ready to detrain in a hurry. Perhaps there were a few soldiers who got off with me when the train paused briefly, but I remember standing all alone beside the tracks as the train started up again, in my high heels and red college girl suit, with the rifle range directly to the west and the entrance to the Fort across the tracks and the highway to the east of me. Soldiers were lying on their bellies firing at targets on the dunes near the ocean; the noise was terrible and the wind was blowing mercilessly, I wobbled and stumbled across the tracks and the highway until I reached the Visitors' Entrance Gate where Ed had left notice of my arrival. I was given directions to the Guest House and teetered along the street crowded with jeeps, trucks, and whistling G.I.s and up the hill to the converted barracks building where I would spend the next two nights. The room was Spartan but adequate and had a view of the parade ground and the sand dunes. The noise of the rifles was muted by the whistling wind.

I memorized some more nerves and muscles, making up my own mnemonics, until Ed came to take me to supper. It was heaven to be held and kissed again but there really wasn't any good place to do more than that. I was a virgin and Ed thought I should stay that way until we married. But mainly we were terrified of pregnancy and didn't know any reliable way to prevent it. So mostly we touched and talked. Ed showed me the lab where he worked and introduced me to some of his fellow workers but I felt very shy and school girlish and didn't know what to say.

The next day Ed had to work so I walked around the part of the Fort where civilians were permitted, then went back to studying in my room. The wind was howling again, around the corners of the barracks guest house, and the view towards the ocean was cold and grey. I was bored and a little scared; the wind seemed to be chastising me for lying to my parents and threatening me with some sort of retribution. Finally, Ed showed up and we had another happy evening but I think he had to be back to bed check by 10 to 11:00. Sunday we spent some more time together but I had to catch the train back about noon. This time Ed stood with me beside the tracks while the train paused and waved me "Goodbye" as we left. I was very glad I had come.

Toting my suitcase back across San Francisco Bay and up the hill to my house, I began to get more and more worried about my lie. I came in the front door and saw my mother and father sitting in the living roon reading. They looked at me without smiling and the air in the room felt very cold and heavy. "Where have you been?" said my mother, in her chilliest Boston accent.

I tried to carry on my lie about visiting Lynn but my mother cut me off and said she had phoned Lynn's family to see how I was and they had never heard of me or my supposed visit. I had greatly underestimated my mother's sleuthing ability. So I had to confess but I assured my parents that Ed and I had done nothing "wrong". My mother claimed she was more worried about my lying to them than about my loss of virginity but I was forbidden to visit Ed again without my mother as chaperone. When I wrote to Ed about my misadventure he wrote back a wonderful letter to my parents telling them how much he loved and respected me and would not do anything to damage those feelings. My father was impressed and told me "That's the way a woman is supposed to make a man feel!"

When I got another chance to visit Fort Ord, my mother drove me there in her 1941 Plymouth and kept an eye on me and Ed most of the time. But she was kind or careless enough to lend us the car to go driving around while she stayed in the Guest House, so we had our own moveable love nest. I learned to tell my mother much more foolproof lies and I got an A on the Anatomy test, but howling wind still upsets me.

II

Marriage
&
Other Adventures

1943-1989

July 25, 1943. 20th birthday.

ARMY BRIDE I

I was married on my twentieth birthday because that was the only time Ed could get a three day pass from Fort Lewis. He was a Ninety Day Wonder, recently graduated from O.C.S. in Fargo, North Dakota, and was teaching Basic Training at the Fort Lewis Reception Center. He was supposed to deliver some troops to somewhere in Texas and would be allowed to stop over in Berkeley on his way back north. I had recently graduated from Cal and had never lived anywhere except the beautiful Ivory Tower in the Berkeley Hills where I grew up.

Ed had found us a honeymoon cottage about halfway between Tacoma and Fort Lewis, one of a row of summer rentals known as the DeKoven Cottages, on Steilacoom Lake. He had also bought a dignified black 1936 Buick for a couple of hundred dollars, from a G.I. who was being shipped out, so he could commute to the Base. Three of the other five cottages were also occupied by new Second Lieutenants and their brides, so I had instant companions. Mary, Betty and Peggy were from various towns in. Middle America and were not a bit like the girls I knew in Berkeley. They were all a little older than I and seemed to have a lot more experience in the ways of the world. They wore quite a lot of makeup, read magazines like True Confessions (which I had soon tired of in high school) and used slang words I didn't know, especially words having to do with sex and going to the bathroom. I had seen a couple of these words written on walls or sidewalks and knew they were "dirty" but I had never heard anyone use them and I had to get Ed to tell me what they meant.

Still, all three young women were lively and kind and I learned a lot from them.

Our husbands carpooled to the Fort whenever they could but often we were left stranded at Steilacoom Lake with not much to do. I learned about housekeeping, home decorating without spending any money, cooking and grocery shoppings-skills I had neglected to acquire while plowing through a triple science major in college. Sometimes we walked to the small shopping center which was less than a mile through pleasant tree shaded summer home tracts. I learned the best bargains in meat to spend my ration coupons on and how to make a casserole — a dish which we almost never had back home because my father didn't like foods "mixed up." Ed was my main cooking teacher, though; he had been away from home for seven years and he had learned a lot from his mother before he left. He taught me to make tamale pie, a favorite dish of his, but I never got terribly fond of it — too much mushy corn meal. He made a great lemon meringue pie, also his favorite, but I never mastered making the crust.

My sister, who had been married four years by then and had also had to learn housekeeping on her own, had given me a wonderful book — something about "1000 Handy Hints for Happy Homemaking." This bible had charts showing how to remove various kinds of stains, instructions for washing various types of clothing, tables for baking and roasting times and schedules for how often to clean various things and with what. Of course, I also had Better Homes and Gardens Cookbook and I always read the monthly features in the Ladies' Home Journal called "This is How I keep House".

Life as a bride wasn't all work, though. During that first summer the three other girls and I spent many afternoons on the little boat dock just down the slope from the cabins. The water was pretty cold for swimming but we worked on our tans, read magazines, made enviously snide remarks about the local residents and vacationers showing off in their boats and talked about our husbands. In September we managed to get the use of one of the cars for three days, pooled our gas coupons and took a trip to Mt. Rainier. We stayed in the grand old lodge, thrilled at the spectacular views of the mountain — more awe inspiring than anything I had yet seen in the Sierras — and had a lot of fun playing in the patches of snow.

Betty, Peggy and Mary also taught me to play bridge. I had managed to get through college and sorority membership without it, mostly because I had a three hour science lab almost every afternoon. The very first time I played, at Betty's house, I managed to win some sort of token prize, I guess because my partners were good players. I also learned about bridge parties.

You have to have a little dish of nuts and one of mints on the table or close by and tall, tinted highball glasses. Sometimes there are celery sticks. Afterwards you serve coffee and a rich dessert you made yourself which everyone exclaims over and says, "Oh, I shouldn't" but has another piece anyway.

Ed was good at bridge and sometimes we played couples. The three husbands were not like any men I had known before, either, but we all got along although the short, dark one Betty's husband tended to get touchy when he had too much to drink. One night, not long after Ed and I had arrived at DeKoven, the other couples surprised us with a shivaree. I had never heard of such a thing but we were serenaded with suggestive songs and told naughty jokes, most of which Ed had to explain to me later. When the celebration was over and it was time for us to go to bed we found a large carrot and two onions arranged on the bed in an unmistakable configuration.

Not all of our social life was with our neighbors. We went to the Officers' Club for dinner and dancing and I got to dress

OVERCOMING CHILDHOOD ADVANTAGES

up in my old college formals which I hadn't used much in college. Ed was a wonderful dancer and I also got to meet and dance with other young officers, some married, some not, from all over the country. It was like making up for some of the fun I had missed while rushing through high school, with the advantage of being a safely married woman. Liquor was rationed and Washington was a bottleshop state so we had to bring our own booze but we tried a little of everything. I never could learn to like Scotch or rum and CocaCola but I developed a taste for Cointreau, Creme de Cacao and Creme de Menthe for special occasions and bourbon and ginger ale for ordinary feeling good tipsiness. Wine and beer were not in style there.

At that time, Fort Lewis was known as the "Country Club of the Army" and I was enjoying it so much I didn't spend much time worrying about what was happening overseas. Ed was classified Limited Service because of asthma and extremely flat feet and it was very unlikely that he would be sent into combat or even near it. One evening we were invited to a party by one of Ed's superior officers. Ed considered this man an "old fart" but, of course, we had to go. He and his wife lived off the Post, also, in a rented ranch style house not far from where we lived. I fretted a lot about what to wear; I didn't seem to have anything between jeans or pleated skirts and formals except a black beaded cocktail dress which I saved for very special occasions. I finally settled on my blue gabardine going-away suit with the padded shoulders and a plain white blouse. I could just as well have worn my bobby sox and saddle shoes, too, because when we got to the party all the women, many of whom were old enough to be my mother, were wearing bright, stylish dresses and lots of flashy jewelry. I looked and felt like a schoolgirl. I have no idea what we talked about — I think I said almost nothing — but the Major kept the drinks and snacks coming and the conversation got fairly loud, especially among the men. At some point, the Major excused himself, saying he had to take a leak (even I could figure out what that meant) and went to the bathroom in the hall just opposite the living room. He left the door open, banged the seat up, pissed a long, loud stream and returned to the conversation. I was very embarrassed but no one else seemed to be.

Our cottage at Steilacoom Lake was my first attempt at nest building. It had a small front room with a fireplace which was our only heat, a narrow dark kitchen and two tiny bedrooms. There was no furniture except the stove and refrigerator but Ed had bought a handsome maple bedroom set from a departing officer for $90. It barely fit into the bedroom with room enough for us to slide around it and get to the closet. The other bedroom was used to store trunks and suitcases as there was no garage. We somehow acquired two, rattan basket chairs for sitting in front of the fire and I made a coffee table by covering one of Ed's foot lockers with ruffled, flowered chintz — something I learned from the other brides. We had the standard student bookcase of bricks and boards but dining furniture was a problem. Ed managed to promote a couple of straight chairs from the Army but we were eating off the top of a barrel. Then a large, mysterious wedding gift was delivered to us which turned out to be a good strong card table. I thought it was just about the best present we received.

Other wedding gifts kept dribbling in, some useful, most not. I was particularly puzzled by a fancy silver object from one of my mother's friends. One side up it looked like an ornate shallow dish on a slender eight inch pedestal but I couldn't imagine what you put in it. My family had nothing like that; they liked Chinese celadon and porcelain dishes with enameled pewter for fancy stuff. The other side up this present looked like a candlestick except there was no good place to stick a candle. I had to write a thank-you note so I referred to it simply as "your lovely gift." Later, some wiser woman told me it was a fruit compote but I had to look up "compote." We used it to keep odds and ends in, like loose change, keys, rubber bands and safety pins but it tipped over easily and tarnished quickly so it was soon stored away.

Our cottage wasn't insulated and as winter weather came on it got very cold. Luckily, Ed could get plenty of heavy Army blankets (I think we had six on the bed) but the blankets and our woolly night wear made lovemaking awkward. We kept the fire going a good deal of the time and still had to wear jackets and long johns when we weren't in bed. I had managed to make, by hand, some curtains for the windows but when the wind blew the curtains did, too, and the candles I insisted on having on the supper table for romantic atmosphere would flicker dangerously.

Driving the ten or twelve miles to the Fort when the roads were icy was a scary business. Once when I was going in with Ed to shop at the PX, we skidded around in a circle, along with several other cars doing the same thing. Miraculously, no one hit anyone else. After Christmas, Ed heard that a small house would soon be available on the Post. It was a regular house with an oil furnace, insulation, new appliances and a lawn which was maintained by the German POW's. We moved in as soon as it was vacant and ended the hazardous commuting. Soon after that I went to work at my first job, as a lab technician for the Army lab nearby. I did tests for syphilis, malaria and pregnancy (a favorite way for WACs to avoid being sent overseas) and began learning how to combine my role as a bride with that of working wife.

Army Bride II

We moved from our honeymoon cottage on Steilacoom Lake to the married officers' apartments at Fort Lewis. Now we had four times as much space, with heating, insulation, two bathrooms and a left-behind sofa and drapes. There were three bedrooms on the second floor and a large basement with set tubs and a work bench so Ed could set up a workshop. We added to our upward mobility by buying a 1931 Hudson so I could have the Buick while Ed was at work. Our apartment was the middle one of five, all identical, in a big, old brick building. There were three more such buildings on the other three sides of the central, shared quadrangle where the clotheslines, garbage cans and carports were. To the East, West and North of us were more quadrangles of brick apartments but our view to the South was of the rifle range.

Most of the time there were trainees on the rifle range, firing their guns and NCOs bellowing orders. Our lawns were mowed and our garbage collected by German POWs who rode in a truck with two guards who were holding rifles. I soon began to understand that the War was more than blackout curtains, ration books and horrible headlines about places I never heard of. One of the German prisoners, an officer whom Ed had gotten to know and respect while he was working in the POW camp, hung himself in his room. A few others had escaped and were either recaptured or disappeared into the wilds of Washington where they were rumored to be living with traitorous local women.

OVERCOMING CHILDHOOD ADVANTAGES

One Sunday afternoon, Ed and I took a walk across the now quiet rifle range and up the steep bluff on its far side, We scrambled through underbrush and woods and came out on an open ridge overlooking the rifle range and the apartments. To our surprise, there was a parade gathering on the big empty field, young soldiers bearing guns, flags or band instruments. As they marched down the field far below us, playing something stirring and patriotic, I was embarrassed to find tears in my eyes. I had thought I was too sophisticated and cynical to be moved by such a sight.

We felt very fortunate to have such a comfortable and spacious new home but I missed the beauty and quiet of Steilacoom Lake and the friendships of the women I knew there. I knew my next door neighbors in the apartments only by the arguments, thumps, crying babies and flushing toilets I heard through our shared walls. There was one woman I had met several times at the clotheslines. She was older than most of us brides and was a Regular Army wife. She was used to moving a lot and told me stories about some of the awful places (Fort Sill, Oklahoma and Fargo, North Dakota) where her husband had been stationed. Finally, she invited me to her apartment for coffee.

Her husband was away but we were met by her small, yappy dog. She showed me her apartment, which was different from mine only in being on the end of the building and thus having more windows. There was very little furniture but in all the rooms except her bedroom there were puddles and piles of dog excrement scattered around on the bare hardwood floors and I had to step very carefully. She could see that I found this distasteful and explained that there was no point in trying to keep Army housing nice. The Army was used to things being left in a mess and would send in a crew to clean up before the next tenant. When she moved into this place, the whole apartment had smelled like a goat because the previous occupants had kept one in their basement to feed their baby, who was allergic to cow's milk. I was so disgusted I didn't go to see that woman anymore, nor did she invite me.

It wasn't long before I was feeling lonely and bored and Ed and I decided that I should go to work. I got an interview with the Commanding Officer of the Ninth Service Command Laboratory and was hired as a GS1 at $110 a month. I wasn't a real lab technician but I had had a lot of courses in chemistry, bacteriology and protozoology so I was allowed to do tests for syphilis and malaria, the latter being common in G.I.s returning from the South Pacific. I also became proficient at doing pregnancy tests for WACs who had either been careless or were hoping to avoid overseas service.

After awhile I was put in charge of the test animals. I learned how to get the rats and guinea pigs in and out of their cages without getting bitten but the rabbits used for pregnancy tests were a trickier matter. They could kick powerfully and scratch painfully and had to be confined in special boxes with only their heads sticking out while I injected WAC urine into a blood vessel in the ear. In the early days of using this "rabbit test" the animal had to be killed in order to inspect its ovaries for swelling, which meant a positive test, but fortunately I didn't have to do that. One time a rabbit died of shock when I was struggling to get it into the holding box and I felt responsible and sad.

Most of the people working at the lab were women but there were two young men in the chemistry section, one a GI and the other a 4F Conscientious Objector. We had a lot of fun, especially at lunch time when we all brought bag lunches and ate together in the Lab. I was discovering the power and elation of flirting while being safely married. I was a little ashamed about it but I knew Ed didn't run away from the admiration of the opposite sex, either. We used 95% alcohol in the Chem Lab for various tests and one lunchtime my coworkers decided it would be a lark to get a lab rat drunk. I had access to the animal house so I provided the rat and the two young men squirted some alcohol between its jaws. It wasn't long before the rat was staggering around glassy eyed and we found this hilarious, though I felt guilty afterwards.

Ed had worked in an Army lab himself and knew there was plenty of high proof alcohol available so he asked me to bring some home. I did so, a little at a time so it wouldn't be noticed, until we had at least a quart. Ed had read a recipe for making Triple Sec and he put the alcohol in a large glass jar, suspended an orange in a hairnet over it and put the lid on tight. The jar sat in our kitchen for six weeks, then he removed the orange, added a thick sugar syrup to the alcohol and we had Triple Sec, of a sort. The best part, though, was the orange, which was so saturated with alcohol that it fell apart at the touch. Each orange section was as good as a stiff drink.

We had lost our DeKoven Cottages friends by moving, but after a couple of months we met two other young couples who occupied nearby apartments and whose backgrounds were enough like ours that we had more in common. We became good friends and took turns having bridge parties for each other. After having been invited to dinner at each couple's apartment, I got up my courage to reciprocate. I had never cooked dinner for company before, but Ed encouraged and helped me and we brought off a simple meal.

When Thanksgiving came, I felt bold enough to offer to roast a duck with chestnut dressing (something I had read about in my delightful new cookbook, *How to Cook a Wolf* by M.F.K. Fisher), while the other couples would bring the rest of the food. On the big day I brought out the cookbook and started to work. Ed had cleaned and trussed the duck and gone off to do something else. Dinner wasn't till 2:00 and all I had to do was make the stuffing and roast the bird. M.F.K. Fisher said I must shell and skin the chestnuts before boiling them but she didn't say how to do this. When I cracked the shells with a hammer or pliers they shattered into small pieces which had to be picked off, one by one. The skin, also, clung to the nut meats maddeningly but it was tough and bitter and had to come off, one shred at a time. After two hours of this, my fingers were sore, I was mad at Ed for not being there to rescue me and on the edge of tears, but I had enough mutilated chestnuts to make the dressing. When I finally had the bird stuffed and in the oven I called the other wives to say I couldn't possibly be ready by 2:00 and to slow down their preparations. Then I had a glass of sherry.

Later in the afternoon, when everyone had arrived with their good looking, good smelling contributions, I took the duck out of the oven for Ed to carve. It smelled good but looked dark and shrivelled. The others made the appropriate appreciative comments but I thought it tasted both dry and oily. The chestnut dressing was really quite good, in spite of a few stray bits of shell and skin, but I resolved never to make it or to roast duck again.

After six months or so of learning to be both a lab technician and a hostess, an unplanned pregnancy (what was then called a diaphragm baby) changed my life completely.

First Pregnancy

When the Army doctor I went to see for my queasy stomach told me I was pregnant, I couldn't believe it. "But I've been using a diaphragm," I objected. The doctor laughed and said, "Half of the women who come in here tell me that. We call it having a "diaphragm baby." I hadn't planned to get pregnant for four or five years. I was just 21 and needed to learn more about myself and about the world outside academia. Besides, I was enjoying being a sort of co-ed bride and a baby didn't fit into that picture. Ed displayed equanimity if not great enthusiasm over my news, though I doubt he felt ready to be a father yet, and so I started studying for a new role.

The prenatal care program at the Base Hospital was pretty simple: Walk two miles a day and don't gain more than 15 pounds, since this was a firstborn. Nothing about stopping smoking or drinking so I kept on with those bad habits and nothing about a special diet or vitamins, though my sister, who was pregnant with her third child and had already lost a tooth, told me to take extra calcium. No classes about pregnancy or childbirth.

So I began to read baby books and magazines instead of marital advise and recipes. My mother sent me Gesell and Ilg's *The First Five Years* which described just what to expect of your baby's development every three months during that time span. "At nine months, the infant will transfer an object from one hand to the other, attempt to pull itself to a standing position and engage in repetitive vocalizing of sounds." (What if your baby didn't do those things at the right time?!) The only babies I had seen were my sister's two and those only briefly. I also bought the *Better Homes and Gardens Baby Book* which gave specific How to and What to Do directions about feeding schedules, crying behavior, colic and other distressing problems. It would be more than two years before Dr. Spock's book liberated me from schedules and expectations and gave me a whole new approach to motherhood.

We bought a crib, a screened foldup affair with a screened top called a PortaCrib, and I began to make lists and to gather tiny garments and diapers. A departing Army wife sold us a nice baby buggy for a low price. I was soon too thick in the waist to wear my jeans or pleated skirts so I had to go looking for maternity clothes which in those days were anything but stylish. They were usually flimsy cotton print dresses with extra material in the front and ties around (or above) the waist to adjust the fullness. They always had ruffles or lace trim on the top which was supposed to draw attention away from the lower part of the body. A far remove from my college wardrobe, but there were not even maternity pants then.

Obviously, I was no longer in shape to be the belle of the Officers' Club so I started creating fantasies about being a lovely young mother wheeling her darling baby in its new buggy. People would stop and exclaim over the perfection of the baby and the youthfulness of the mother.

For a month or so I enjoyed my two mile walks around the Base. I could walk through the brick Married Officers' Quarters, speculating on the domestic lives of my peers, on to the PX for groceries, around the main entrance circle where all the trucks full of troops and the jeeps full of officers seemed to keep flowing in an endless stream and back by the rifle range to see how the sharpshooters were doing. We acquired a small, pretty collie mix, named Mabel by Ed though I would have preferred something more literary and romantic, who accompanied me on my rounds. But soon it began to rain a lot, almost every day. I bought a yellow slicker which hid my expanding middle and a yellow sou'wester hat which looked pretty cute, I thought. Some of the soldiers going by in trucks thought so, too, and I got some gratifying whistles as long as my shape was hidden. I also got some knee-high rubber boots in which I enjoyed stomping through the puddles like a kid. I couldn't get the boots off by myself, so Ed made me a sturdy wooden bootjack which worked fine. Still, walking was a cold, damp business and Mabel was much less eager to accompany me.

Toward Spring, Mabel ran off without me for a walk one day. I called and called but didn't know where to look. Later in the day, an M.P. came to my door to tell me that she had been killed by a truck down by the Circle. Mabel had been my closest companion for almost six months; I took care of her, nursed her after she was spayed, talked to her and petted her during the long, boring days and occasional nights when Ed was gone. Somehow, I felt responsible for her death — I should have tied her up or kept her in the house — and I went into a depression that lasted several weeks. But the baby was kicking harder all the time, what looked like knobby little knees or elbows poking sharply out of my huge round belly, and it wasn't long before the living displaced the dead in my thoughts and feelings.

The rule about gaining only 15 pounds was more difficult to follow than the one about walking. I was five foot seven and slender but I had a healthy appetite and it wasn't many months before I was almost up to my weight limit. It was rumored that if you went over the limit the Army doctor wouldn't let you have your baby in the hospital there. We really couldn't afford to pay for private care or to drive to Tacoma for it. The Army doctor put me on a very strict diet and for the last two or three months of my pregnancy I can't remember eating anything except lettuce, tomatoes and cottage cheese, Apparently the diet was not good for my body chemistry because one day in my eighth month I got a nosebleed that wouldn't stop. I lay in the bed surrounded by blood soaked towels and a wastebasket full of bloody Kleenex and toilet paper. Every time I thought I had it stopped and tried to get up, it started again. Ed was away, delivering troops or prisoners somewhere, I knew my mother was coming, by chance, later in the day. She was working for the Red Cross as a psychiatric social worker at the Veteran's Hospital in Walla Walla, across the state. (Meanwhile, my father was doing his patriotic duty by working as an engineer for the Navy, teaching SeaBees on Kodiak Island.)

When my mother finally arrived and saw the bloody mess I was in, she got me to the emergency room pronto. There they cauterized the leaking blood vessel in my nose and sent me home with iron tablets, Vitamin K, and something else to speed clotting time. I couldn't be bleeding like that during delivery!

It was before midnight on a warm June night that my labor started with of rush of amniotic fluid. After Ed got me to the hospital he was told to go home and wait till he was called. He joked about this being a good chance for him to look up a friendly WAC he knew but I didn't find that funny. I was scared and in pain and there were no books then to teach women about the stages of labor or how to help the process along. I was left all alone, in a narrow room in a narrow bed with side bars like a crib with a nurse checking on me occasionally. The nurse was pretty bored with the whole thing and would tell me only that I still had "a long way to go." Finally, the pains got so bad — like no other pain I had ever experienced or imagined — that I couldn't help crying out. I called for my mother and then for God in whom I had not believed since I was 12. I felt ashamed for making such a fuss, especially when the nurse came in and told me to quiet down.

Finally, after six hours or so, they decided I was ready to go to the delivery room but as my feet were being strapped in the stirrups and my arms strapped to my body, at ether mask was put over my nose. I knew nothing more until I woke up in a ward with several other women and was told I had a healthy, 8 ½ pound baby girl. (So much for my diet keeping birth weight down.) Then Ed came out grinning proudly even though he had said he wanted our first to be a boy named Jonathon. Soon our daughter, Joanna, was brought in. She was a miracle with lots of dark hair, a red face and the ordinary number of fingers and toes. But I had never seen a newborn before and it seemed to me that her head was a funny shape — long and narrow and sort of squashed. The nurse reassured me that wouldn't last but it worried me anyway.

At that time, 1945, new mothers had to stay in bed in the hospital for ten days. On the ninth day we were allowed to sit on the edge of the bed and dangle our feet, and on the tenth day we could stand on the floor and take a few steps if our legs weren't atrophied from disuse by then. (But the entire medical expense for my Army baby was $10.00 for my food in the hospital) I was finding nursing messy but very satisfying so feeding the baby at home would be easy but I had very little strength or energy, after 10 days in bed, for other housekeeping activities. Luckily, my mother had been able to get leave from the Red Cross to take care of me and the baby as I was stuck on the second floor of our house for another 10 days until I was allowed to go up and down stairs.

Having my mother there meant almost immediate conflict over when to feed the baby, how long to let her cry, how many clothes to put on her and how much fresh air and orange juice she needed. I wasn't able yet to stand up to my mother but Ed had his own ideas about baby care and there were some tense moments. Finally, my mother had to go back to work and Ed and I were left alone with Joanna to begin the long, painful, exhilarating process of learning to be good parents and learning to accommodate to each other's ideas of what that meant.

Baby Makes Three

When I was born my grandmother lived with us, so she helped my mother take care of me and run the household. I also had a baby nurse for several months. When my daughter Joanna was born I was on my own, far from home with no one to give me advice or babysit. My experience with infants consisted of holding my sister's firstborn for a few minutes. Ed entered enthusiastically into his new role as father, diapering, comforting and entertaining Joanna, but he was gone all day. Since I was nursing, he couldn't feed her so I got all the night duty. I was trying to follow Gesell and Ilg's *The First Five Years* and the *Better Homes and Gardens Baby Book* schedules for feeding and sleeping times, but Joanna didn't want to wait four hours between nursings and her sleep patterns didn't follow the book at all.

Sometimes I would let her cry for awhile — it was supposed to be healthy exercise for her lungs — but often I couldn't stand it for long and would pick her up and walk and talk to her until I couldn't stall her any longer and gave her the milk she wanted. Then I worried that I was spoiling her. The first few months, I had so much milk that she used to almost choke on it as it came spurting out, which probably made her colicky. The strict diet I was on during pregnancy had not kept her birthweight small but it had caused me to lose about 20 pounds so I was very slender except for my big leaky boobs. For the first and only time in my life, my bust measurement was larger than my hip measurement! I smelled milky most of the time and had to change my blouse several times a day, not just because of my dripping breasts but because Joanna spit up a lot. I got so I could burp her on my shoulder and wipe up sour milk from the floor at the same time.

The Book said the baby should take long naps in the morning and afternoon and sleep 10-12 hours at night by 6 weeks of age but Joanna hadn't read the book. She did pretty well with the daytime naps unless outside noises awakened her and I got so I guarded those nap times like a dragon; they were the only times I had to get much housework done or have a little rest. Nothing and nobody was allowed to interfere with those naps. The noise from the rifle range was far enough away that it didn't seem to bother her but I remember sticking my head out of an upstairs window and scolding some children making innocent noise in the courtyard below, then feeling like an old grouch. No matter how short a nap she had, Joanna always woke just before supper and that was her social time. I learned to make dinner preparations with one arm if Ed wasn't home yet and to eat while holding a fussy baby. We didn't have a rocking chair but we had learned that she fell asleep when riding in the car so I would put her in her buggy and toll it back and forth over a stick with one hand while I ate with the other. If she started to cry, I'd roll the buggy faster and faster, bumpetybump, until she quieted. It was a long ways from a romantic dinner for two.

Whether her naps were long or short, Joanna always woke again just as we were going to bed. I know many attempts at lovemaking were abruptly ended when a whole different set of my hormones was called into action by Joanna's crying. One night, after a few months of solitary night feedings Ed asked me as I crawled back into bed, "Which do you like better, having a baby or being pregnant?" I loved my baby and was very proud to have her but when I thought back to the fun and freedom I'd had while pregnant, all I could say was, "Wait and ask me when I've had her for nine months so I can compare better."

I don't know why I couldn't get either of our bridge playing women friends to babysit for me. Maybe their husbands had been transferred by then or they were scared of babies or were having too much fun at the Officers' Club. We tried playing bridge a few times, both in our own home and at our friends', taking Joanna along in her basket. But she always woke up before the game was over and had to be passed around from one dummy to another and we had to haul along the PortACrib or play pen which was a big hassle. One time we tried taking her to a dance and left her sleeping in her basket in the car just outside the door. But I was worried about her and had to keep checking on her so often we finally gave up and went home.

At last, we found someone willing to babysit: Bob, a lonely bachelor friend of Ed, whom we had to supper several times and who enjoyed playing with Joanna. We excitedly planned a big evening at the Officers' Club. I had bought a breast pump and painfully pumped off a bottle of milk to leave behind with Bob who assured us he could manage just fine. I made sure Joanna was asleep before we left and I had a wonderful time, dancing in the old formal that fit me again. But when we got home two or three hours later, Bob was walking the floor with a screaming Joanna and looking harassed. She didn't like her milk in a bottle and had been telling him so for quite a while. I felt so bad about putting our friend through that ordeal I never asked him to sit again, but later, after Joanna was weaned, we made friends with an older, childless couple who sat for us several times.

Grocery shopping was a problem for me, too. There were no handy cloth or plastic baby carriers in those days. You either carried the infant in your arms or left it in a safe place where it couldn't roll off. The PX grocery carts had no place for an infant and no carry-out boys. How to manage several bags of groceries and a tiny baby with only my two arms? One day I arrived at the PX with Joanna asleep in her basket in the back seat. IT was a warm, sunny day so I cracked the window a bit, arranged a blanket in it to shade the baby's head and left her sleeping while whirlwind shopping. (No kidnapping worries then.) When I returned to the car ten minutes later, there were five or six people gathered around it and Joanna was screaming lustily. These were middle-aged people, all old enough to be my parents, and they scolded me harshly for leaving the baby alone. One woman told me I should be turned in to authorities for child neglect. I felt that I had been a really terrible mother and I never left Joanna like that again. Of course, none of these people offered to hold her for me while I shopped.

Diapers were another big chore: I had to wash them by hand in the kitchen sink and, because Joanna had sensitive skin and kept getting a rash on her bottom, I had to rinse them several times, once in a solution of baking soda, and dry them in the sun whenever possible. In the winter, this meant that they freeze-dried on the line into stiff rectangles and had to be thawed out on racks in the house.

My milk supply dwindled after about six months and I had to start the formula and bottle routine. The formula was made up of canned Carnations or Pet milk, Karo and boiled water in unvarying proportions. The eight bottles had to be sterilized every day in a big speckled blue enamelware steamer before being filled. I don't know why the pediatricians insisted on this routine then. Joanna spent a good deal of time scooting around on the floor putting everything she saw in her mouth, but I followed the sterile bottle routine religiously. Bathing the baby was also a strict routine and had to be done every day at the same time unless the baby was sick.

Still, we had a lot of fun with Joanna and marveled at her

development; I proudly recorded every step in her progress in the Baby Book, which of course, confirmed our opinion that she was a superior child. She was cute to look at and we took hundreds of pictures. She had become my new career as "perfect mother".

Joanna was just two months old when the bomb was dropped on Hiroshima. Of course, Ed and I were glad the war would end soon but we were appalled and frightened by this use of atomic energy. I knew about the tests in New Mexico but hadn't realized that the A-Bomb was actually going to be used on people. Now I felt that the world would never be the same again. I remember sitting out on our patch of lawn with my baby on that warm, soft August evening, waiting for Ed to get home while my neighbors were celebrating and I was thinking mostly dire and troubling thoughts about the future.

It was six months before Ed had accumulated enough "points" to be discharged and he struggled with what to do with his life after four years in the Army. He had been drafted right after he graduated from college and had little work experience in his field of biology. He wanted to start a marine lab, collecting and supplying specimens to schools and colleges, like the admirable Doc Ricketts of Steinbeck's *Sea of Cortez* but we didn't have the needed capital. He considered staying in the Army but I was against that.

My parents were back in Berkeley and said we could stay with them while Ed went back to Cal on the G.I. Bill so that's where we headed.

The Army moved all our household possessions to storage in Berkeley and we loaded our '36 Buick for the long drive south. I was worried about traveling for three days with an active 8 month old baby and the disruption of my carefully established routines. We packed the back of the car level with the seat, covered all with the crib mattress and so had a giant playpen for Joanna. I was adamant about daily baths and sterilizing of bottles (Boy, was I dumb!) so we spent two nights on the road at housekeeping motels where I could satisfy my need for sanitation. And so I arrived back in Berkeley 2 ½ years after I left it and a quite different person from that love-struck college girl.

Fort Lewis, Washington.

Joanna at 2 weeks.

Mabel.

Joanna, 1 month.

Starting Civilian Life

After Ed was discharged from the Army, in February, 1946, we returned with our eight month old daughter, Joanna, from Fort Lewis, Washington to my family home in Berkeley. It was two and one half years since I had left and I was a different person. My grandmother was now living alone in Carmel, my sister was a faculty wife with two babies in Berkeley, my father was back from Navy duty in Kodiak and reopening his office at home, my mother was still with the Red Cross but was stationed at the Naval Hospital in Oakland, working with physically and mentally damaged veterans. There were a couple of tenants renting rooms in the big house but my mother arranged for me and Ed and Joanna to have the largest bedroom and we all ate our meals together.

At the University, Ed was advised to give up his dream of opening a biological supply lab and to go into teaching, a field where there was a great demand. He had his BA in Biology and could get a high school credential with one semester and a couple of summer sessions. So he started classes at once and began applying for jobs. Of course, I was hoping he could get work someplace in the Bay Area but the offers came in from places like Crescent City, Coalinga and Salinas. We finally chose Salinas and, with the help of the high school, found a brand new duplex on the (then) outskirts of town at the edge of the broccoli fields. (The house is still there, across form the Northridge Mall.)

We moved into the house in August with two rattan basket chairs donated by my parents, a wooden barrel for a lamp table and our footlocker turned coffee table. We had out secondhand bedroom set from Fort Lewis (which I am still using) and Joanna's baby furniture. The kitchen had a stove and a fridge but we actually went out and bought a new kitchen table and chairs at Monkey Wards — our first purchase of new household furniture. But the most exciting purchase for me was a washing machine. I had been washing all our clothes, including the diapers, in the sink or laundry tub and my new Kenmore was like a gift from Heaven: It was a wringer type, of course, filled by a hose from the wash tubs, but it made my life so much easier. The landlord had put in plenty of clotheslines and unless it was foggy, there was usually a strong breeze to get things dry.

Of course I had to be sure there was not disking or harvesting happening on the other side of the fence or the clothes would be coated in dust.

We had the back half of the duplex so the view from the living room was of the driveway and the other duplexes; the kitchen and back bedroom looked out on the double garage and a newly planted expanse of weedy green lawn where the long strings of clotheslines were stretched near the five foot fence which separated us from the broccoli fields beyond. The front of the duplex was occupied by another high school teacher, Bob, a large, stocky, balding man who taught Industrial Arts; his wife, Virginia, who was a warm, cozy epitome of domesticity; and their little boy, John, who was about Joanna's age. They were kind, friendly people but we didn't have many interests in common other than out children and school doings.

Bob and Virginia's bedroom backed right up against ours and we often heard rhythmic squeaking and thumps coming from the other side of the wall. We giggled and made sure our bed didn't touch the wall or have any squeaky parts but this was a common interest we didn't talk about with our neighbors.

Joanna and John played well together and soon we had a wading pool in our driveway (the lawn was too new to stand the traffic) and the neighborhood playgroup of one-and-a-half to four year olds. Virginia and I took turns keeping an eye on things or, if we weren't too busy, sat together for shared observations and comments. Our street was a real danger at harvest times when huge trucks roared along it into the fields, then back again loaded with lettuce or broccoli. The rest of the year it was a pretty quiet street except when the men drove off to work in the mornings and when they returned again at suppertime. None of us young families had second cars so the women and children were stranded at home unless we took our husbands to work and picked them up afterwards. Ed and Bob took turns driving whenever they could but that didn't work if one or the other of them had to stay after school to coach a sport or go to a meeting.

Ed's and my social life was spent entirely with other teachers or at school events. We went to potlucks, bridge games and school bazaars. If Salinas had any classical music or theater events, we were not aware of them. We and our neighbors babysat for each other occasionally which worked nicely except when we were all supposed to attend the same school function. I learned that, as a high school teacher's wife in a smallish farm town, I was expected to dress and behave in a manner beyond reproach; never smoke in public or appear in shorts, jeans, or lowcut blouses. No getting tipsy at parties or dancing too close. It was well known that the male teachers who smoked at school (I doubt if any female had the nerve) went out behind the shop buildings at recess and lunchtime but the authorities chose to ignore this breach of propriety.

The only women's group I could find to socialize with was the AAUW which also consisted mainly of teachers' wives. Actually, I found it a pretty dull bunch, inclined to take itself too seriously. We had earnest but uninspiring speakers on various state, national and foreign dilemmas as well as occasional bake sales and raffles to raise funds for worthy local causes like scholarships and libraries. Once I won a booby prize in a raffle; it was a one-way train ticket to Chualar, a tiny farmworkers town about twenty miles down the track. It was the equivalent of going to Podunk. I never used the ticket but I was glad that someone in the AAUW had a sense of humor.

SALINAS

I learned my first hard lesson about budgeting in Salinas. Ed's salary was $2200 a year which was pretty slim for a family of three, even in 1946, especially when more than a quarter of it went for rent. I had saved several hundred dollars of the money I had earned working in Fort Lewis, so when we ran out before the end of the month (which was every month at first) I drew some out of my savings. But I failed to keep track of how much savings I had spent and suddenly the bank informed me that account was overdrawn. I was mortified that I had been such a poor manager! We made an even stricter budget (broccoli or lettuce from over the fence for vegetables, fewer trips in the car, essential purchases only) and Ed got a Saturday job selling menswear at the local Sears store but I still felt I had been a very poor wife.

Joanna was continuing to make me feel like a really proud mother, though. She learned new words every day and could run, jump and climb easily. When I had to go to the grocery store, about three blocks away, across Highway 101, I put her in her stroller — small-wheeled, noisy, unpadded wood and metal go-kart which was nothing like the luxurious, cocoon like, pastel carriages of today. (I suspect the modern versions have built-in bottle warmers and piped in lullabies.) Joanna's stroller had two features: a sturdy strap to keep her in her seat and a little metal tray in front from which she could hurl toys. The foot rest was handy for kicking off her lowcut shoes and dropping them in the middle of the highway as we dodged traffic. In the grocery store, the strap was essential to keep Joanna from climbing out and investigating everything on the shelves. One time, though, as I stood in the narrow aisle pondering which laundry soap to buy, Joanna reached over and knocked a glass bottle of bleach off the shelf. There was a reeking puddle of Chlorox, both breathtaking and nose shriveling. I was totally humiliated but the store people were very nice about cleaning up. I paid for the bleach and, after that, I made sure the stroller was parked outside Joanna's reach of any shelves.

Another shopping problem was taking Joanna to the freezer locker. We had gone together with some other teachers' families and bought a quarter of beef — a much cheaper source of meat than the local butcher shop. The beef was cut to order, packaged and labeled and kept in a walk-in freezer place down the highway. It was so cold in there that Joanna would start to cry even when she was all bundled up. Probably the feeling of claustrophobia when the heavy door shut after us contributed to her fears. I tried leaving her with the attendant in the front office but she cried as soon as I disappeared behind that door into the frigid blast of foggy air. I think Ed finally took over the task, stopping at the freezer on his way home from school but I was never sure he would bring me the cut of meat I asked for, so my menus were rather impromptu.

Winters in Salinas were often cold, foggy and dismal. A cousin in Idaho sent Joanna a hand-me-down snow suit which I stuffed her into when she wanted to play outside. She looked very cute in it but it was a struggle to get it on and off, especially now that I was toilet training her. The first time I can remember yelling at her she must have been about 18 months old. She had just stoutly refused the toilet routine so I tugged the snowsuit on and she went happily out to play — to return in five minutes, needing to go potty. I blew my top, then felt like an utter harpy and an unfit mother.

Part of my toilet training technique was to leave Joanna for a few minutes, sitting on her potty seat until she produced "results." One day she complained of a tummy ache and I knew there had been no "results" for several days. The pediatrician advised an enema and, after several attempts, that treatment produced not only the desired results but copious amounts of undigested toilet paper! Joanna had been pulling it off the roll and eating it to while away her bathroom time.

In spite of these setbacks, we were now feeling confident enough as parents to think about having a second child. My sister's sons were barely two years apart in age and, watching her hectic life, I decided that was too close together. For some reason, I also thought that three years would be too wide a gap and that two and one half years' difference would be perfect. Ed agreed and, to my smug delight and his amazement at our easy fertility, I became pregnant within a month. Our son, Jonathon, was born on January 7, 1948, weighing nearly nine pounds and arriving almost before the doctor could get to the hospital. In fact, the nurses in the delivery room instructed me to keep my knees together and not push, a whole different experience from Joanna's birth. Of course, hospital care changed completely after the war and I was home again in a few days, with Ed's mother to help out. My own mother was recovering from a hysterectomy.

Jonathon's first weeks were frightening ones for me. It was midwinter and I caught the flu, probably at the hospital. I was so afraid of giving it to the baby that I stopped nursing for awhile, pumping off my milk so Ed could bottle feed him. But he got sick, anyway, and I would lie in bed, feverish, listening to his wheezy breathing and tiny, tight coughs and thinking I had killed him. Of course, we both recovered, but he wasn't allowed outside in his buggy, even on a sunny day, until he was two months old. After that, he thrived and weighed almost 30 pounds by the time he was a year old, contributing to my lopsided posture and aching back. By now, though, Ed and I felt like experienced parents (a feeling which did not last) and Jonathon was not subjected to the intense scrutiny and worry his older sister had to go through those early years.

BACK TO BERKELEY / LOOSENING THE MOLD

I was delighted to be back in my home town with its gorgeous views, its disregard for convention, its rich fare of concerts and exhibits and its varied cultural and intellectual stimulation. I had my mother or her part-time housekeeper right next door for babysitting and my sister was just up the hill so we could trade off responsibilities while our kids played together.

Then there was the whole new experience of a coop preschool for me and Joanna, now 4 years old. The school was held in the basement of my childhood elementary school. Since it was under the wing of Adult Ed, mothers attended class one night a week and participated as teacher's helpers one morning a week. In a few months I learned more about raising kids than I had learned from all the books and trial and error methods of the past four years. Here were a lot of other young mothers, many of them my neighbors, dealing with the same problems I was, with two wise and wonderful teachers to guide and reassure us and Dr. Spock as our main reference book. Those of us who lived on Panoramic Hill took turns carpooling the kids to school and then, four mornings a week, we had only stay-at-home infants or toddlers to cope with. Jonathon, at one-and-a-half, couldn't go to preschool yet, but he played happily with his blocks, cars, books and records for long periods with or without the company of his age-mate cousin, Roger.

At school, besides learning applied child psychology, I learned how to make playdough, finger paint and other essentials for entertaining small children. I felt I had been given a reprieve from isolation, boredom, uncertainty, and squirrel cage worrying. Joanna was timid and clingy about school, at first — she had never seen so many children her size together before and some of the boys were rough and boisterous (or just plain mean) but she soon got hooked by all the activities available. The basement of Emerson School was not an attractive place: water pipes, heating ducts and wiring ran along the low ceiling, the few windows were too high to see out of and the overhead lights were glaring. But the instructors had made the area quite pleasant with brightly painted cupboards and bookcases as dividers, pint-sized tables and chairs, and braided rugs.

In the evenings we often invited one or two of Ed's fellow grad students for supper, after which there was much 'learned' conversation, from the emerging Cult of Dianetics to the Korean War, from doctoral candidate hurdles to the meaning of life and the destruction of the planet by the greedy forces of Capitalism. I didn't mind a bit being the only woman in the group, even if it meant listening while refilling cups and glasses a lot of the time. Then there were all the free concerts, old movies, museum shows and art exhibits at the University within walking distance. It was a great life and I felt I was making up for some of the adolescence I had missed by rushing through school and into marriage.

Jonathon did start preschool when he was around 2 ½ and Joanna was by now in Kindergarten, in the same building and at the same hours. It was time for ME to go back to school. I enrolled in the graduate program in Zoology, not so much because I wanted a Master's Degree or had any idea what I could do with it, but because I wanted to be on campus again. After all those child rearing books, courses like "Ecology" and "Bio-Statistics" sounded fascinating. I was assigned to a professor of Parasitology I had had in my undergraduate days. He was a cold, dry little man with thick glasses, a sallow complexion and a pinched nose, who spent his life peering through microscopes at exotic worms and their hosts. My old college text on the subject had a lot of appalling pictures of long tropical worms being drawn out of people's bodies and being wrapped around a stick, gently, so sections wouldn't break off and be left in the person. My kids' favorite picture, though, was of a man with elephantiasis of the scrotum, sitting upon the afflicted part. But what my professor wanted me to do was to look through a microscope for hours at a time at hundreds of snail shells and determine statistically whether the snails with the left spiraling shells or those with right spiraling shells were more certain to harbor a particular parasite. I didn't seem like something I wanted to spend a lot of time on and was probably the beginning of my disillusionment in Science as the Meaning of Life. I settled for just taking classes and hanging out in Ed's office with the other (all male) grad students. They all accepted me as a peer and included me in their jokes and gripes. Even a 26 year old mother of two can enjoy a little harmless flirting, though Ed confided in me that his good friend Bruce, whose wife was still stuck at home with a small baby, had what he called a "married man's crush" on me. I was in a graduate seminar with several of the men and I can't even remember what I was supposed to report on but I was terribly impressed by the subjects the others presented, even if I could barely understand them. There were no other women in the seminar, of course,

 I liked Bruce a lot but I was more attracted to another of Ed's friends, Murray, who was emerging from a messy, painful divorce and who was in my Ecology class. He kept LOOKING at me soulfully across whatever space we were in; Ed and I had been married almost seven years and Ed didn't look at me like that anymore. I took to hanging around places I knew Murray would be just to kid around with him. Ed was often gone doing field work or errands for his professor. His Master's project involved, among other things, a study of the fishery of Lake Temescal with recommendations and implementation of a management plan. (Grad students are a great source of free labor for any government agency; in this case, it was the Oakland Parks Department.) Ed was so busy, so hardworking, responsible and GOOD that, almost thirty-five, he seemed to be getting rather stodgy and settled. He did still make jokes about wanting to find a rich widow to support him but I didn't think they were very funny. (He WAS very attractive to older women.) Murray was just my age and wasn't nearly as serious as Ed — in fact, he was something of a flake about hard work. His Master's project consisted of sitting in the San Francisco Aquarium night after night, staring at tanks full of trout and charting their behavior. He knew a lot about books and music and psychology and introduced me to *The Brothers Karamazov*. He wasn't practical like Ed but he seemed to be more appreciative of culture and to take life more lightly. (I ignored the fact that he wasn't trying to support a wife and 2 kids.)

I was having such a good time on campus that I was neglecting some of my motherly and household chores. One time I got so engrossed in doing some reference work in the biology library that I was a half hour late picking up Joanna at Kindergarten.

She was sitting all alone and completely forlorn on the stairs into the school while the teacher, who had stayed with her — bless that woman — had gone inside to try once more to reach me on the phone. The house was getting very little cleaning and often I didn't fix supper when I should have. Ed would come home and find two hungry, grumpy children and me, sipping a glass of Red Mountain and reading or writing a story. (I had started a correspondence course in writing.) He was amazingly tolerant of this behavior and often helped me cook, but my mother, stopping in after her work day, was less forgiving and bluntly told me to quit stalling and take care of my family! Of course she had outside help and she and my father often went out to dinner.

The male chauvinist who advocated keeping women barefoot and pregnant must never have had to worry about his wife getting Seven Year itch. 1 recognized the symptoms in myself but did nothing to combat them.

Joanna and Grandmother.

Grandfather with Jonathon at 7 months.

Joanna and Chum, 1948.

1952

A CHANGE OF SCENE

We moved from graduate school in Berkeley to the tiny town of Overton, Nevada in June 1951 with our two small children and a fluffy yellow cat they had named Daffy (for Daffodil). Overton was a desert town of 500 Mormons and a few government workers, 65 miles east of Las Vegas where the Virgin River flows into Lake Mead. Ed was hired by Nevada Fish and Game to work on the fishery of the lake.

We rented a small concrete block house, built in the fashion of desert settlers, with the bedrooms in a half cellar and the living area above. There was a huge swamp cooler which blasted dank air to both floors and which we ran day and night most of the summer, when the average daytime highs were 112^0. We parked our blue '48 Dodge in the shade of a giant cottonwood tree but even so I had to keep a pair of gloves in the car because the steering wheel would be too hot to grasp. In the mornings we had iced coffee because the hot kind made us too sweaty, even at 6:30 A.M.

Our front yard consisted of a large, horseshoe-shaped area of devil grass which was watered weekly by the town system of irrigation ditches. The back yard was creosote bush, mesquite and a few teddy bear cholla to keep walkers alert. The sandy soil was baked and encrusted with white salt streaks in jagged patterns. In the distance loomed the pink and gold mesas.

Ed had arrived in Overton before me and was well settled into his new life. His grey Fish and Game uniform included a broad brimmed felt cowboy hat and he bought desert boots to complete his Western ensemble. He was even issued a sidearm to pack in case he met any poachers and had to act as a game warden. He drove a State pickup truck back and forth to the lake and had a State 25 h.p. outboard in which to run around and see how the bass and blue gill were doing. Once, on my way to the lake, I found his pickup lying on its side where he had skidded in the sand, rounding a corner too fast. He was unhurt but I felt as if I scarcely knew him anymore. He seemed to be playing the part of some reckless tough guy.

I was having a much more difficult time adjusting to desert life. I missed the view of San Francisco Bay, the lush gardens, the concerts, the bull sessions with other students, even the fog. The only music on the radio was Country Western and we own very few records. There was no library except the one full of L.D.S. treatises, but I was determinedly plodding through *The Brother Karamazov* which I had started in Berkeley and which seemed to keep me connected to my life there.

Joanna, just six, was improving her reading skills with dozens of comic books and played occasionally with Louise and Eloise, the twins of the Park Ranger. Jonathon, three-and-a-half, played in the irrigation ditch or constructed roads in the dirt for his Dinky cars. Both children were fascinated with the many lizards and the large varied insect life. They knew enough to keep away from the rarely seen gila monsters and scorpions. Ed brought them a tarantula in a jar and a desert tortoise which we tethered to the back porch and fed lettuce. We also had some sand pink sidewinders in the refrigerator, awaiting shipment to the Museum of Vertebrate Zoology in Berkeley. Daffy, the cat was very interested in the insects and reptiles, too, but the heat was hard on her. She would lie under the coolest corner of the house, panting in her long, yellow fur coat.

Shortly after we arrived in town, I was invited to an afternoon get together by the wife of the biologist who was working on desert bighorn sheep. The Demings were Mormons and Mrs. D had invited a number of churchwomen to meet me. Coffee and tea are taboo for L.D.S. so we sipped lemonade and ginger ale and nibbled homemade cookies. I don't think I had ever seen so many flowered print dresses in one room and I felt odd in my denim skirt and white blouse. The talk was of recipes and sewing projects. One of the women asked where I was from and I replied, rather smugly, "Berkeley," believing there was only one city of that name in the nation and that everyone knew where it was. My questioner said, "Ohhh! Berkeley, Idaho?" And began naming the people I might have known or met there. I was embarrassed, I'm not sure now whether for her or for myself.

One of the evening entertainments in the town, other than the third run, weekends-only movie house, was bat fishing. When the bats came swooping after the insects at dusk, some of the local men would get up on the flat roofs of their houses or porches and fly cast for them. When Ed tried it and finally caught one, he didn't know what to do with it. I stared at its ferocious little face and fast fluttering heart until he was able to set it free. The children were excited and sad. We didn't fish for bats anymore.

One day I noticed that Daffy wasn't eating or chasing bugs. She lay around in the box I fixed for her and we thought she must have eaten a poisonous lizard or insect. There were no doctors in Overton — for animals or humans — and we felt scared and helpless. In the morning, I found her dead in her box, her lovely fur flat and dull. The children were not awake yet so I asked Ed to bury her in the desert on his way to the lake. When the children got up, I explained what had happened and the three of us cried together a little. Another of my connections to Berkeley was gone.

OVERCOMING CHILDHOOD ADVANTAGES

Joanna and Jonathon spent the morning playing with a neighbor's new burro while I did laundry on the back porch. After lunch we were due to go to the lake to swim in the bathtublike 85⁰ water which the children loved. I decided to do a dump run on the way. Overton had no garbage service and so we hauled all our trash to a ravine a few miles beyond town. Luckily, things dried out fast in the desert heat so the odor wasn't overwhelming. You could see all sorts of things at the Dump — old tires, broken toys, worn out furniture and clothes, cans, bottles, everything that the citizens of Overton wanted to get rid of in the days before recycling and composting.

I flung my bag of garbage over the edge of the arroyo while the children poked around the discarded toys. As I turned to go back to the ear, my eye was caught by a limp pile of long, fluffy golden fur riffling in the breeze. This was how Ed had "buried" Daffy! I pushed the children into the car before they could see and drove away to the lake, hiding my hurt and anger. It seemed to me that Daffy's end symbolized everything harsh, hostile and alien in this place I was trying to make my home.

We left Overton within a year, when Ed got a job with California Fish and Game. He and I forgave each other for many more serious breaches of trust over the next 40 years, but I don't think I ever forgave him for what he did with Daffy.

Transition

We returned to Southern California and moved back into Ed's parents' rental house. I was hugely pregnant with our third child which we had postponed having while Ed was in graduate school because we were too poor. Martha was the largest of my three babies and grew up to be almost six feet tall.

Ed and I had learned to be more relaxed parents by then so we probably let Martha get away with behaviors we didn't allow in her older siblings — at least, Joanna, seven years older than Martha, accused us of spoiling her younger sister. We did enjoy the baby but Ed decided we couldn't afford to have any more — ever — and got himself a vasectomy for insurance. I was pleased not to have to bother with birth control any longer.

By the time Martha was one-and-a-half we really needed a larger house with three bedrooms and we found one in a working class neighbhorhood in San Pedro, closer to Ed's work at Terminal Island. My grandmother gave us the $3000 for a down-payment and the G.I. Bill took care of the rest of it.

We were comfortable in our new home for about a year, but Fish and Game was sending Ed on collecting and tagging trips down the coast of Baja California and into the Sea of Cortez. Ed kept getting worse and worse sea sickness and finally, on a long trip, he became dangerously dehydrated and had to be rescued by helicopter and brought back to San Pedro.

I'm afraid I wasn't sympathetic enough when he arrived. I

had just been nursing all three children through mumps *and* chicken pox and still had the pox with a fever of 105° myself

Ed immediately requested a transfer to Inland Fisheries and was relocated in Sacramento. We found an old Quonset hut backed up to a drive-in movie theater out in the "suburbs" which was fine while we looked for a more civilized home closer to downtown Sacramento. We found a nice little house "near schools and shopping" and were settled in by the time school started.

We raised our children there for the next sixteen years, by which time we had moved twelve times in the eleven years we had been married. We were very ready to stay in one place for a while.

Four generations.

OVERCOMING CHILDHOOD ADVANTAGES

Salinas, 1949.

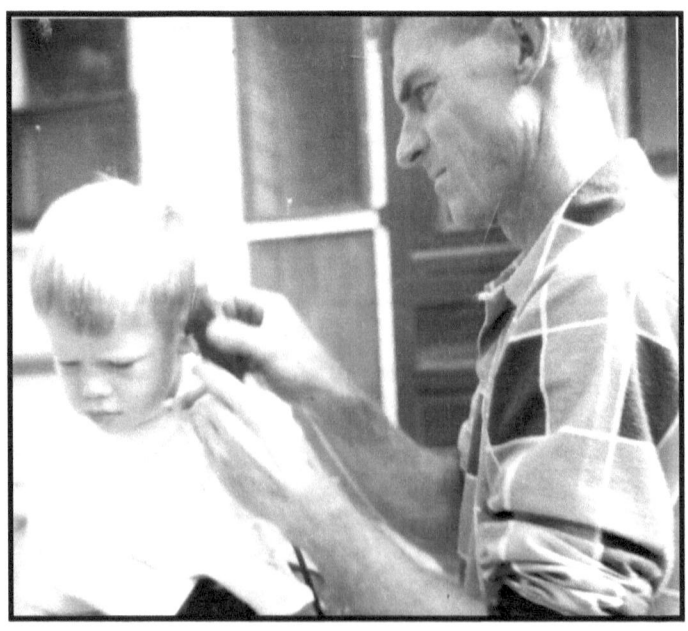

Saving money. Gardena, 1951.

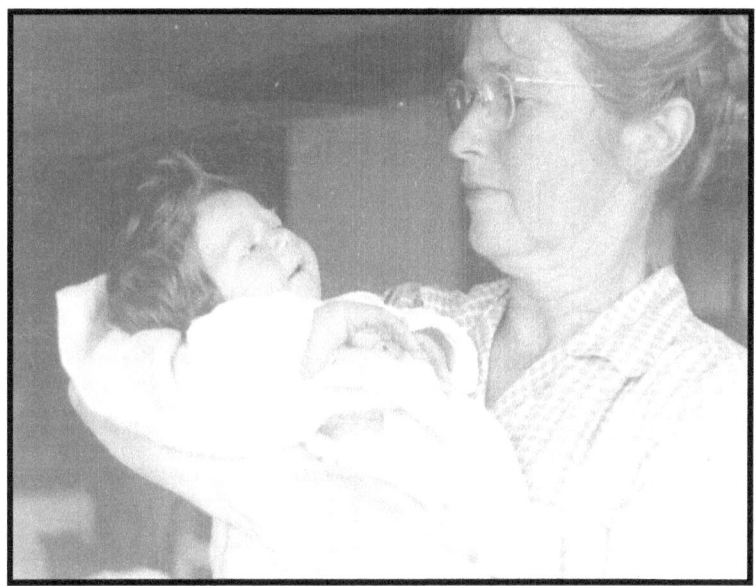

Martha at 1 week, 1952.

 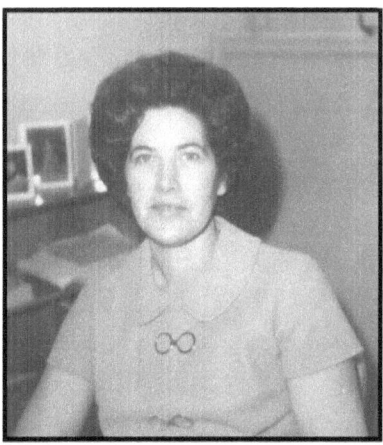

The joys of public service. Ed as a State Fish biologist and Rosalie as a school psychologist.

Feather River Summer

The summer of 1956, when the children were four, eight and eleven, we spent camped in a twenty foot trailer in Plumas County. Ed's job was to find three dam sites in the county where water could be stored for recreation, irrigation and flood control, with minimum damage to the local fishery. The trailer and Ed's pickup truck were provided by the State of California. We brought our old green umbrella tent for the kids to sleep in and our blue '48 Dodge for family transportation.

Ed had found us a place for the summer at a campground near the tiny town of Blairsden, right on a bend of the Feather River. It was a pleasant spot with plenty of space for privacy and trees for shade. We drove in tandem from Sacramento, with Ed in the pickup, towing the Aljo trailer, and the children and me in the Dodge. We were just getting settled in our camp spot when we heard sirens of emergency vehicles coming into the campground. Soon the brush-lined riverbank was being searched by sheriff's deputies, volunteer firemen and grim-faced campers while a mother wailed for her lost toddler. The drowned child was not found until the next day and, for me, it was as if a chilling cloud of threat and fear surrounded our arrival, a cloud which hovered in the background and loomed periodically during the rest of that summer. None of us ever went swimming in that part of the river.

We soon settled into our new camping life. Ed was off in the pickup exploring the back country all day while I did rudimentary housekeeping and took the children on short excursions. Blairsden was O.K. for getting bread or ice cream cones but for serious shopping, laundry or library facilities we went to Portola or even to Quincy, the County Seat. Most of these trips were enjoyable but occasionally something happened that brought back to me that sense of malevolent spirits, lying in wait. Once, as the children and I played in the clear, shallow, sandy bottomed creek near Quincy, Joanna came to me, crying with leeches clinging to her ankles. I ripped the evil, slimy black strips from her legs and stemmed the flow of blood but we left and never swam back there again. Another time, as we picnicked up a dashing, rocky stream far from any help, I heard what I thought was a rattlesnake nearby. At that time I had very little experience of the outdoors. The children were happily building a dam but the rattling sound kept coming closer and finally, in panic, I herded them back to the car and drove away. (I later learned the noise was a cicada.) Then there was the time I unavoidably squashed a chipmunk under the wheels of the Dodge, then burst into tears while the children screamed at me.

My biggest fright happened when I finally gave in to eleven year old Joanna's entreaties to go for a horseback ride. We found an out-of-the-way spot offering rides — just a private barn with a few horses, really — and the owner led forth a ten-foot high horse he assured me was gentle and tractable which would, he said, just go around a loop and return to me on its own. Joanna was put in the saddle, looking thrilled, and then the owner persuaded me to let Jonathon (then eight-and-a-half) ride behind and hold onto his sister. "No extra charge," he said. Off they went, along the dirt road into the trees, but the horse starting jouncing and Jonathon flew off the back end and lay, absolutely still on his back in the road. I believed I had caused him to be paralyzed for life but he just had the breath knocked out of him. I can't even remember if Joanna got to have the rest of her ride but we didn't go near any more horses that summer.

There were some practical problems associated with camping, too. Taking baths was one of them. There was no washhouse at the campground so we took a lot of spitbaths and did a lot of swimming but once in a while we needed shampoos and scrubbing with soap. Ed made arrangements with the campground manager to use the bathroom in one of the unoccupied summer cottages on the property. The children and I would get all our clean clothes and washing supplies together, get the house key from the manager, and troop through the woods to the empty cabin. I think by then the children were refusing to get in the same bathtub together (there was no shower) so that meant three or four low level baths in succession so as not to drain the small hot water tank. Then we all traipsed back to camp while I nagged the kids to keep their damp towels out of the dirt and to avoid poison oak.

Mostly, I was alone with children but we did have two sets of visitors that summer. My parents came up from Berkeley for a few days, stayed in the Blairsden Inn, admired the beautiful scenery and were very polite about our living conditions. And our neighbors from Sacramento came with their two children — Mark, who was Jonathon's best friend back home and Wendy, who was a little younger than our four-year-old Martha. We made the five kids play outside while we four adults drank beer and fixed supper in the tiny trailer kitchen, But then it began to rain, HARD, and the nine of us had to spend a long evening wedged in together in space designed for four. Before long, it became obvious that we adults had little in common except our children's friendship. I think the rain finally let up enough so the children could go to bed in the tent but by after breakfast the next morning we were more than ready to be without company again.

The last two weeks of the summer we moved the trailer to Taylorsville, another tiny town closer to where Ed needed to work for that time. The only place to park it was in the yard of some kindly forest ranger, near his barn. I remember almost nothing about the spot except that the town had a public swimming pool where we could take showers. And one day we met a road worker who had been bitten on the arm by a rattlesnake and had driven himself to the hospital, forty minutes away. It was the first time I heard that rattlesnake bites were not inevitably fatal!

We were all glad to get back to Sacramento in time for school in the fall. We had missed our suburban friends and routines and activities but I had learned one more way of adapting to change. Since them I have become an expert at camping and at dealing with rattlesnakes on the trail, headstrong horses, leeches, dead chipmunks, ticks, backpacking in the rain and taking a bath in a bucket. But I am still haunted by the drowned toddler and when I take my grandkids camping near the water I keep a very close eye on them.

OVERCOMING CHILDHOOD ADVANTAGES

Sacramento, 1954.

Sacramento, 1952.

Christmas Card, 1953.

Back To The Land

The town of Petaca was not on our AAA map, though it was in the part of New Mexico made famous by Georgia O'Keefe and Maria, the maker of black pottery. We followed our daughter's directions and turned off the paved road at Ojo Caliente, a dilapidated hot springs resort about halfway between Taos and Espanola, in the Rio Grande Gorge. A well graded gravel road led us up into evergreen forest, with surprise views of the wild mountains around us and an occasional dwelling or small farm. We were at 7000 feet elevation but our new turquoise pickup purred along easily, even laden with our rented cab-over camper. Ed and I had a month's vacation from our jobs to visit our eldest and her man and to take in some Western scenery along the way. We'd been on the road from Sacramento for three nights and were still trying to get used to the cramped living space of the camper.

It was the summer of '70 and Joanna and Cleve had fled Berkeley some months earlier to become New Mexico Hippies — though they never used that term, preferring to call themselves and their friends "freaks". After spending some time in a commune near Chimayo, they had used Cleve's insurance money, $500, to buy an acre of land with an old schoolhouse on it near Petaca. I was longing to see Joanna after so many months of worry and minimal communication but I was also apprehensive about the meeting. Our daughter might be a stranger to me! We found the place to turn off the gravel road and bounced down a rutted dirt track, across a fenced field of weeds, to a flat bank above a small river. We knew we were in the right place because Joanna's car was parked there — the dark green '58 Chevy sedan, formerly a Forest Ranger's car, which Ed had given her for her graduation from Cal the previous year. The little adobe house was on the other side of the river and up the slope, the only bridge being a flat log for foot traffic. Soon Joanna and Cleve were greeting us lovingly and taking us on a tour of their property; The dry, rocky land between the river and the house had been cultivated by hand and planted with corn, beans, tomatoes, potatoes, many kinds of greens and marijuana. Since it was too cold to plant anything at this altitude until June, things were just beginning to be ready to harvest. Joanna carried all the water for this one acre garden, pail by pail, up from the Tusas River, the flow for which was controlled by a communal irrigation system — like the one in *Milagro Beanfield Wars.* There was also a well near where we had parked, on the far side of the log bridge. I can't imagine that any of this water would have passed Health Department inspection for potability but we had not yet heard of Giardia in those days; we all drank it and, miraculously, did not get sick. The adobe school house had been divided into three rooms a big kitchen-eating area, a living room which was rarely used because it had only a worn piece of rug for furnishings and was too big to heat comfortably, and behind this a six by ten foot sleeping area which was small enough to be heated by two bodies in close proximity. The kitchen was where the action was; there was an enormous old wood burning stove which had a tank on the side for hot water and which provided all the heat for the house (there were freezing temperatures and snow any time from October through May). There was a rickety table and chairs, shelves and boxes for kitchen supplies and even a record player on a small side table. It was a portable player which we had sent Joanna, knowing how much she must be missing listening to music. Unfortunately, the resident goat, which often came in the house, had climbed up on the player, trying to get at food on the table, and had squashed the player. The bantam hen and rooster were like pets, too, and came and went through the unscreened window or door whenever they pleased. The official pets were two Siamese cats which Cleve and Joanna had gotten as kittens from some fellow freaks. The female, Frog, was small and jumpy and looked like the creature for which she was named. The male, Baby, was a very large, virile tom who was mellow and sweet tempered when not confronted with another tomcat. Both cats tolerated the goat and the bantams. The other livestock included about a dozen White Leghorns which were kept outside in the fenced in ruins of an adobe chicken house, a grey horse named Tesuque who seemed to be around mainly for atmosphere, and an untamed pony which Joanna had gentled enough to accept a bridle and which she sometimes rode to the Post Office to get the twice a week mail. The only other important feature of the property was the outhouse which was about as far up the sagebrush slope above the house as the house was above the river. The outhouse tended to be inhabited by spiders and bees in the daytime but, thanks to the regular use of lime, was not an unpleasant place to visit, briefly. Old catalog pages served as toilet paper.

 Real toilet paper was used in the house as a substitute for every other type of paper product — tissues, napkins, towels — because it was so much cheaper. A roll sat on the dining table, near the stove and beside the bed. The other function of a bathroom, bathing — was accomplished by heating a large washtub of water on the stove and, at least in the summertime, hauling it out behind the house where Cleve had built a sort of leafy screen where one could bathe with some privacy. Our tour was complete and it was time to present the gifts we had brought for our pioneers: a fifty pound sack of brown rice, a treadle sewing machine for Joanna and an old rifle for Cleve — for hunting rabbits and deer. Everything was greatly appreciated and we sat around, drinking beer and watching the sun drop below the darkening mountains while Joanna built up the fire in the big range and began preparing a stew for dinner. I didn't even know she could cook but she had not only learned how to make delicious, inexpensive meals she had learned the art of cooking on a woodstove — a very different skill from cooking with gas or electricity. She could also swing a mean axe for chopping wood and splitting kindling. Where had she learned all these skills? Certainly not in suburban Sacramento or in the Art Department at U.C. Berkeley! That night, the starry sky was an incredible sight and we crawled into our camper, happy that we had come. We spent two weeks in Petaca, sharing Joanna and Cleve's daily routines there and learning about their lives. It was a town which had been founded by the Spanish, 400 years earlier, and descendants of the original families still lived there, raising cows and horses and doing mainly subsistence farming. But now Hippies had invaded the valley and coexistence with the old settlers was not always comfortable. The Jaramillo brothers, who lived across the road from Joanna and Cleve, were friendly in a superficial way but I got the feeling that their "neighborly advice" was more like a warning or disguised threat. One day I drove Joanna to the nearby town of La Madera, where she had learned substitute teachers were needed (a job for which she met the requirements) but she was told that Anglos need not apply. And when we went to the grocery store for emergency supplies (all they had was beer and pop, canned goods and Wonder Bread, but the supermarket was an hour away) we rarely got a friendly look or word. Joanna's '58 chevy was not running because of some needed part not presently available or affordable. Ditto for Cleve's '48 Dodge truck. So Ed and Cleve took the camper off of our pickup, leaving our little home standing on its hydraulic jacks for the remainder of our visit, looking quite unsteady, though it was perfectly safe. All four of us were able to squeeze into the wide front seat of the pickup so we went to Espanola for a big shopping expedition and then to Taos for exposure to Art, Culture, tourism and spectacular scenery. One day a rattlesnake came into the garden; Joanna found one of the cats about to pounce on its coiled-up form. I was terrified and demanded that Cleve kill it but he demurred, saying it was the snake's territory first — a point of view I had not heard before and did not, at that time, subscribe to. After that, I was very cautious about walking around outside.

I helped haul pails of water for the garden, fed the chickens and the goat, learned something about how to cook on a woodstove but never tried chopping wood. The longer we were there, the more I noticed that Joanna was doing all the work while Cleve smoked dope, read, brooded or contemplated whatever graduates in Philosophy contemplate. That made me angry and when it was time to leave, I was ready. Besides, the discomforts and inconveniences of our stay were beginning to outweigh the fun and adventure. Ed and I went on to the wonders of Mesa Verde and Yellowstone, then back to our easy, busy lives in Sacramento. That winter Joanna and Cleve were arrested and jailed for growing marijuana. Joanna suffered a miscarriage in jail. They were finally released on condition that they immediately return to California, where they would be placed on probation for a year. They had to sell or give away all their animals, except the cats, and leave behind everything they had dreamed of and worked so hard to achieve. We were able to let them move into our rental cottage in Carmel, where Joanna got a job in a pizza place and Cleve did odd jobs when he felt like it. The following summer, when Ed and I went to

Santa Fe for a workshop, we stopped off in Petaca and retrieved the sewing machine which, miraculously, was still standing in the little adobe house — even though the house had been broken into and occupied by drifters. A few months later Cleve, wanting cash for a car, sold the property, for the $500 he had paid for it, to a shoe salesman from Albuquerque who wanted to put a vacation house on it. The Hippie era was over, at least for Joanna and Cleve, and, though they had a daughter born in the Carmel cottage, their relationship ended soon after.

House in Petaca

Joanna and Cleve

First Grandchild

The phone call from my son came in the middle of a busy morning of report writing in my Sacramento office. Jonathon's voice, telling me of the birth of his son, was so filled with pride and joy that I, too, felt elated, all doubts about his readiness to be a father swept away.

Jonathon was 24 and had dropped out of U.C. Berkeley in 1968, at the end of his junior year. He had been living above Moe's bookstore on Telegraph Avenue, in what was jokingly referred to as the Telly Hilton, had been manhandled and teargassed by police and had witnessed the People's Park shooting from the rooftop of his building. He hated the Vietnam War and thought it unfair that college students were deferred while less fortunate men were drafted. Besides, he was smoking a lot of dope and failing a class in architecture. He and his love, Mary Ann, had gone to live in the hills above Garberville, in Humboldt County, where it was easier to avoid the Draft. A friend whose wealthy Corning Glass father had given her ten acres of land there, was inviting people to come and settle on her property. Jonathon and Mary Ann had our old green canvas umbrella tent, our old, reliable and dangerous Coleman gasoline camp stove and a brown 1948 Chevy panel body truck which could be driven to within a mile of their tent site, if rain had not made the dirt road impassable. Winters they spent in a communal house in Berkeley where Jonathon worked at short-term jobs: pumping gas, delivering packages, stripping furniture. Mary Ann may have been getting unemployment for a while and then welfare but they had no other visible income. I don't know how they saved any money for the times when he wasn't working. When they announced that a baby was due in April of '72, I was dismayed!

But now, their son had arrived, born in the back of the panel truck in the Humbolt hills, an hour from the nearest doctor with Jonathon as the midwife. Jon had walked three miles to the nearest phone to tell me the news. He sounded so thrilled that I forgot all my misgivings. But then he said, "The baby's got a little problem — a split lip — but otherwise he's fine. We're calling him Buddha Roy. And Mary Ann is fine, too."

A cleft palate! Certainly not from Jonathon's side of the family; nor from Mary Ann's side, Jon said. He called it "instant karma." I did not get to see Buddha Roy until he was two months old and by then he was a big, bouncing baby with golden curls and skin the lovely *cafe au lait* color that can come from having parents of different races. I had not held a little baby for almost 20 years and had forgotten the wonderful, warm, heavy, trusting cuddle of a sleepy infant, the milky, powdery smells, the satiny skin, the tiny fingers that could grab and hang on so tight, the coos and gurgles — and the kicks and screams, the arms and legs that go stiff when you want them to bend, the dirty diapers. Roy was a perfect baby except for his hare lip which began at his left nostril, distorting his nose slightly, and extended through his upper lip and part of his palate, just left of center. The gap was an inverted "V", exposing his gum, but seemed to give him no trouble nursing or babbling.

Very carefully, I asked my son what could be done to repair the gap. He told me they would do nothing until Roy was old enough to be weaned, as surgery would make nursing impossible and would be too traumatic for an infant. His reasons sounded right, and yet I found it hard to have a grandson who was less than perfect physically. I did not take many pictures of Roy and always tried to take them from his undamaged side.

When he was ten months old, Roy had his first lip surgery at Children's Hospital in Oakland. He and Jon and Mary Ann were living in a tiny house, one step above a hovel, in Richmond — on Mary Ann's A.F.D.C. and Jon's odd jobs. It was a very hard time for all of them. Jonathon was harassed by the black men living in the neighborhood for being with a black woman — something he had not experienced before in liberal Berkeley or hippie Humboldt. Roy cried a great deal because he could not nurse and would not accept a bottle and Mary Ann felt the loss of the nursing connection as keenly as her baby. I did not think the surgeon had done a good job; there was still a lot of lumpy scar tissue on Roy's lip and his nose was still out of shape. Jon told me there would be another surgery later to improve Roy's appearance.

That summer, the family was back in the Humboldt hills where Jon was building a cabin on his corner of land. He scavenged lumber and trucked it to the end of the dirt road, then hauled it on his back, a timber at a time, the mile into his building site. My husband and I visited them there, sleeping uncomfortably in the back of our pickup truck at the end of the road. They had a beautiful vegetable garden, watered by PVC pipe running from nearby Tom Long Creek, and were able to trade veggies for an occasional fish or chicken. There were lots of wild blackberries and some abandoned apple orchards in the hills. They had Food Stamps and earned some cash (and some of the crop) by harvesting and grooming pot plants grown by other residents of the property. Roy was thriving in the outdoors, in spite of being dirty most of the time. He had loving attentive parents, though I thought they could have told him "no" a little more often. I was proud of my grandson's sunny nature, strong body and amazing vocabulary. The whole family seemed healthy and happy in their tiny, unfinished, one room shack but I wished they were living more conventional lives back in Berkeley.

Then there began to be trouble in Hippie Heaven: someone O.D.'d on Angel Dust and had to be taken to the County Hospital Emergency Room in Eureka; the marijuana crop was raided and a big source of income disappeared; the woman who owned the land lost a lover and attempted suicide; and Jonathon fell and broke a rib, which landed him in the hospital with a punctured lung and pleurisy. He and his family made it back to the Bay area, where they camped out for a while in his garage, but the cabin was never finished and they never really lived in the hills again. Jonathon had managed to escape the Draft for five years and now the Vietnam War was ending and he no longer needed to worry.

When Roy was three years old, his sister, Delia, was born, in a funky backyard cottage in southwest Berkeley. Jonathon was away for the day but returned in time to help deliver the baby and cut the twisted cord, while Roy played in the next room. There were no problems; Delia was a perfectly formed little girl, with the same lovely, tan skin as Roy but with a head of kinky black curls. For this arrival, though, we received no thrilling telephone announcement. We drove from Sacramento to Berkeley for a visit and there she was, two days old already!

High School Grads.

OVERCOMING CHILDHOOD ADVANTAGES

Jonathon in the 1960's.

Joanna when a teenager.

A Season of Change

Ed knew, before I did, that we needed to change our lives. He was 54 and his job in the State bureaucracy under Governor Reagan's regime was growing increasingly frustrating. I was 7 years younger and just hitting my stride in my new career as a school psychologist. Our two older children had fled the bland Dick and Jane suburban Sacramento life we had so carefully created for them, as soon as they finished high school and now our youngest was about to take off for college on her own.

For several months before that summer of 1970, Ed had thought the answer to his dissatisfaction was another woman and when I found out about her we almost fell apart. But 26 years of loving connection had made a bond too strong to break and now we were learning how to stay together more comfortably and openly. We spent a lot of time at Esalen, learning Gestalt therapy, bioenergetics, massage, Tai Chi, group dynamics and about ourselves and our relationship to each other.

Our older daughter had managed to graduate from Cal the previous summer, in spite of the Free Speech Movement, the shootings in People's Park, the teargassing of Vietnam protestors and the assassinations. After a year as ice cream truck driver and mail carrier, she had fallen in love and, with her man, Cleve, headed for a commune in New Mexico with the $900 Cleve had lifted from a dope dealer acquaintance.

Our son, though, had succumbed to the Summer of Love

and the drug scene in Berkeley and had dropped out of architecture school after his third year. He and his lady love were camping in the hills of Humboldt County, spending winters in a communal house in Berkeley where he could earn a little money at odd jobs and she could collect unemployment. I was still struggling with the guilt of "What have I done wrong?"

Ed loved to make things and fix things. His garage full of tools and gadgets was as large as our two bedroom plus den home and he always had a project under way. He decided he wanted to learn blacksmithing — ornamental iron work, not horseshoeing — and began reading books and magazines, going to observe blacksmiths, collecting tools, and finally trying it for himself on weekends in places like Sutter's Fort and the County historical park. By summer, he had decided on early retirement and had arranged a less responsible job for himself during his last year of State employment so that he could spend more time on his new passion. He found an ad in a metalworking magazine for a blacksmith school in Santa Fe, New Mexico and got a six week vacation so he could attend the school that summer.

Meanwhile, I'd been learning to weave in order to keep pace with the Age of Aquarius. I really enjoyed my new hobby and felt I was freeing my creative spirit at last. We made arrangements for me to take weaving and ceramics at St. John's College in Santa Fe, while Ed was at blacksmith school, and got a room in the dorms there. Leaving our home in charge of our eighteen year old daughter (a mistake) we headed off in Ed's new pickup to begin our groovy, new life.

St. John's College was on a hill overlooking Santa Fe, with a lovely view of desert and mountains. There were not many summer students and the dorm we were assigned to was almost empty. We got a large, corner room intended for four students and rearranged it for ourselves, with two of the beds pushed together. My first purchase in Santa Fe was not some arty, expensive, (possibly) Native American creation but kingsize bedding to hold our beds together and thus continue the binding and healing of our conjugal wounds.

The Summer School Dean reminded me of Dragon Lady. She told me about the Weaving and Pottery classes I had signed up for but seemed mostly interested in the payment of our fees. I had also requested a class in Conversational Spanish, but since the College did not offer that during summer session, Dragon Lady had arranged for a tutor for me — a young local man, Luis, who, she assured me, would be very helpful. We set up when and where I was to meet him and how much I should pay him. We were given meal tickets for the cafeteria, told the rules about lights out, quiet hours, smoking and other prohibitions and were ready to start our new experience.

Turley Forge, where Ed and three other students (all much younger than he) were to spend 8 hours a day, 6 days a week learning the art of blacksmithing, was down the hill and across town, so if I needed the pickup for errands or explorations I had to deliver Ed there at 8:00 a.m. and pick him up, all sooty, grimy and sweaty, at 5:00. Quite a bit of the time I was not in classes I spent in the laundromat. I liked Weaving class a lot: we built small frame looms for making Navaho style pieces but I had also brought my eight inch sample loom which could weave more intricate four harness patterns. The class, which numbered only half a dozen women, drove to Albuquerque one day to pick out yarns and raw wool for those who wanted to learn spinning. Pottery class was less successful. I was still trying to learn to throw on the wheel but everything more than three inches in diameter came out lopsided.

My Spanish tutor was a handsome young Latino of about twenty. I don't know how he had managed to convince the St. John's Summer School Director that he was qualified to teach

Spanish. He certainly knew street Spanish — Pachuco, it was called then in Southern California — but he had no concept or knowledge of grammar, no parts of speech or verb tenses or syntax. I had had a year or so of conventional night school Spanish so I had some vocabulary and was trying to learn the past tense. But Luis seemed unfamiliar with the verb forms I wanted and he corrected my pronunciation so it would sound like Pachuco. Some of this was interesting from the point of view of studying local idiom but I didn't think it would help me back in Santa Cruz County or even as a tourist in Mexico.

Not only did Luis and I have trouble communicating in Spanish, he seemed to misinterpret what I said in English, also. We met for our lessons on one of the quiet balconies of the college library, where you could sit and talk undisturbed. Luis would pull his chair very close to mine, put his hand on my arm to make a point and look deep into my eyes. I believe he thought I was a rich, bored, lonely *gringa* who wanted a gigolo and he was offering himself in that capacity. I couldn't really understand what he was saying but after about a dozen lessons, during which I learned no useful Spanish and grew increasingly uncomfortable in his presence, I told him I didn't want to continue.

That summer was a period of adjustment in my marriage, as well as in my relationship to the larger world. Ed had, with great difficulty, decided to end his affair with the other Woman and stay with me. We were treating each other very carefully and lovingly, rebuilding trust, but I knew he still thought about Rudy and sometimes sad and angry feelings got the best of me. Rudy had been more involved with counterculture ways than I and I identified some of Ed's new interests and beliefs with her influence. He had been playing with trance work, astrology, mysticism, Tarot cards and past lives.

One evening we were sitting in the lounge with a couple of

young student dorm mates. One of them had a Tarot deck and knew how to read the cards. She offered to do a reading for Ed and he entered into it enthusiastically. As each card was laid out and interpreted by the reader, he seemed to find what she had to say really important and relevant to his life. With my long scientific training, I thought the whole performance bizarre, ludicrous mumbo jumbo and was appalled that Ed seemed to believe it. When the last card was turned and the last solemn prediction made, I could stand it no longer. I believed Ed was listening and accepting with the mind-set he had learned from Rudy and her hippie psychobabble. I quickly left the room, with no explanation, and ran out into the warm, soft, sage-brush scented star spangled night. I walked fast down the hill toward Santa Fe, till I could feel some of my fury dissipating with the night breeze as it dried my damp skin.

It was about an hour before I climbed slowly back up the hill and entered our dorm room, feeling defensive about my irrational behavior but still very cool toward my husband. Ed greeted me with bewilderment and concern and I tried to explain my reaction to the Tarot reading without mentioning its connection in my mind with Rudy. He gave me warmth and reassurance but let me know that he found this other world interesting and worth exploring, even if he did not believe in all its precepts. As far as I know, he never had another Tarot reading, but as I mellowed through the seventies, I had one, as well as experiencing the *I Ching,* palm reading, horoscopes, spirit guides, ESP, and dream interpretation. I don't believe any of these systems influenced the life decisions I made then but they were fun to speculate about.

By the end of that summer, when we returned to Sacramento and the world of work, I was feeling a lot more comfortable with Ed, reassured of his love for me and able to let him explore beyond the Doors occasionally. I ventured with him now and then but, mostly, I remained grounded in my job and my family. He set up a blacksmith shop downtown and became utterly enthralled with the down-to-earth hard work of shaping iron into beautiful and useful objects. After three years of supporting this creative but financially losing endeavor, I grew tired of my unrewarding job and quit, before retirement age. We left Sacramento forever, as poor for a few years as when we were first married, living in rented trailers, cramped cabins and even a converted garage as we drifted from Point Reyes to Santa Cruz. Finally, we were able to buy an old house in Aptos in 1976 and lived there happily until Ed's sudden death in 1989, never regretting the changes we made beginning in the summer of '70.

Dropping Out With a Safety Net, 1975

When Ed and I decided to quit our jobs and follow our children's example into a simpler life, it meant that our income dropped from that of comfortable middle level professionals to what it was in the early days of our marriage, struggling along on the G.I. Bill. I could not collect retirement for four more years and Ed's retirement was very small, so we had to find ways to cut expenses. We still had one child in college, but she was twenty-one, having spent two years doing her own dropout thing, and we knew she could support herself without any help from us. We cleared out our home in Sacramento, where we had spent twenty years working and raising our children, stored what we did not want to sell and could not give away, then rented the house for enough to pay our rent elsewhere. We were moving to Inverness because we wanted to be on the coast and because Ed had a part-time job, at minimum pay, as a demonstration blacksmith at Point Reyes National Seashore. He had done blacksmithing at Sutter's Fort and at the Wawona History Center as well as for three years in his own shop since his retirement and he was not only a good ornamental iron worker but a great ham at playing the part of a turn of the century smith. The visitors loved him, especially the kids, when he let them turn the handle of the blower or make a horseshoe nail. We found a tiny cottage near White House Pool, at the end of Tomales Bay, with a garage-shop space big enough for Ed's many projects and a glassed in front porch big enough for my thirty-six inch loom. The cottage was up a steep gravel road, hidden in oak and madrone trees, and suited our desire for privacy. Fitting our big hideabed couch (for guests) into the living room and our old double bed into the bedroom were real challenges. (The kingsize bed we loved had to be put in storage.) I learned to cook and heat with propane and almost got over being afraid that the big blue tank would blow up on me. We ate a lot of beans and pasta and bought the few clothes we needed at thrift stores. Medical care, thanks to Kaiser, was free but almost an hour away in San Rafael. Shopping at the Palace Market in Point Reyes Station was cheaper than at the Inverness Store, where the nearby Yacht Club and the long tradition of summer homes for Berkeley professors and retired military meant for a higher-priced economy. We discovered most of the people near our age were part of this upscale scene while the other dropouts tended to be much younger and into homegrown sprouts, tofu, organic vegies, meditation, Tai Chi and astrology. We tried all these things and more but found most difficult to commit to completely. The young people were polite to us old hippies, a few even sought our advice, but they didn't invite us to their parties any more than the Yacht Club Gang did.

 The other kinds of people we saw around town were the hardworking Italian-Swiss dairy farmers who had been out on that windblown point for generations and were not about to be chummy with Park Ranger or transient types, and the residents of the nearby Synanon Ranch who came to town (in supervised groups) to shop. The women were especially easy to spot because of their shaved heads and long old-fashioned dresses. Ed and I had visited the Ranch a few years earlier when our niece was married, along with fifty other brides and grooms, to the man she had met in a Synanon therapy group in Los Angeles. The compound was in a beautiful setting, at the old

Marconi estate overlooking Tomales Bay, but it was run like a medieval fortress. Our niece and her husband and baby had left when the child was six months old, the age at which babies were required to be placed and cared for in the communal nursery where their parents were allowed to visit them only once a week.

In Sacramento, our social life had been based on friendships with coworkers and longtime neighbors. In Inverness we had neither and I soon found I was very lonely. Several of our friends had promised to visit us in our new home in this famous vacation spot but none of them ever came, few even wrote more than once or twice, and I felt abandoned. During the summer season, Ed worked most days at the Park where he had plenty of contact with both visitors and staff. I had no one to talk to except clerks in the grocery store and the librarian and I decided to volunteer at the Park Visitor Center. I got to make reservations for the hike-in camp grounds, answer questions from the many visitors and sell books and postcards. I also got to wear a special green and gold vest and patch which proclaimed me a V.I.P. or Volunteer in Parks. I enjoyed my role and it gave me lots of social contact but I did get tired of telling people where the bathrooms were and why they couldn't park their RVs on the beach. After the summer was over, though, I was needed only on weekends at the Visitor Center and that left me with lots of time to fill. Ed always had some repair or building project going on out in his workshop so I began designing and weaving large, ambitious garments — all ungraceful when finished and scratchy to wear. I also started hiking all over the National Seashore, from one end to the other, as much as 10 or 12 miles a hike. Sometimes Ed would drop me off at one end of my trek and pick me up hours later at the other. He had a bad foot and could not hike far. I loved watching the red tail hawks and surprising deer, rabbits, raccoons, sea lions and other wild creatures and just enjoying the scenery, the solitude the physical challenge. I'd never done any physical exercise before. The discovery that I could disappear for hours and still get myself home again on my own two feet was exhilarating. Walking and weaving were like twin meditations for me. When I was home, weaving or not, I listened to music a lot, both classical and the folk rock of the day. I had had a very short adolescence and now I allowed myself to form sentimental attachments to songs by Carly Simon. James Taylor, Carol King. Cat Stevens, Crosby, Stills and Nash, Judy Collins, as well as my old favorites — the Beatles, the Stones, Joan Baez, Bob Dylan. Ed was tolerant of my pop music infatuation but I turned it off if he was in the house for long.

When it got too rainy to walk every day, I started a yoga class at the Dance Palace, the cultural center of Point Reyes Station. There were no movies or other entertainments closer than San Rafael or Petaluma, almost an hour away over dark, winding two lane roads. The Dance Palace was a large, ancient, wood frame building on the main street of the town, which is Highway One. It may have once been a hotel where dances were held but now it was the community center for everything from town meetings to self-improvement classes to performances by local musicians or theater groups. Television reception in the area was abysmal (there was no cable) so the Dance Palace doings were usually the best way to spend a Friday or Saturday night. I didn't make any lasting friends in the yoga class but at least I got to talk to some women, most of whom were younger and more flexible than I.

In the early spring, after what seemed like months of rain and fog, Ed was told that the Park had no more funds for a demonstration blacksmith and, in fact, would have to close the blacksmith shop in preparation for building a big, new Visitor Center. He puttered around in his garage workshop for a while but soon grew restless and announced he wanted to explore job possibilities and living places in Santa Cruz County, a retirement option we had talked about earlier. I was willing to move but we had a year's lease on the house we were in, which did not run out for four more months. We couldn't afford to pay rent in two places but Ed thought he could live in our thirteen foot travel trailer until he found work and a room to stay in. I was to remain alone in Inverness till our lease ran out while he got settled and found a place to rent that we could afford and that would be available at that time. I was very angry at being deserted in a place where I had no friends and few social activities but I was stuck or believed myself to be. While I fumed and fretted through that spring, Ed hauled our little house trailer to the Golden Torch Trailer Park on Freedom Boulevard where I visited him for one uncomfortable weekend. But soon he found friends, handyman jobs, and a free place to stay through our fellow Unitarians. He was very good at household repairs, had his pickup for tools and hauling, and was soon much in demand. Finally, when our lease was up in June, he came back to help me pack and move our stuff. We had moved ourselves with rented trucks before but it was a strenuous and stressful chore and I was still smarting from being left. The house which Ed had found for us to rent, near the Yacht Harbor, would not be available for several weeks after we had to vacate the Inverness place so we had to store a lot of our things and squat in a converted garage belonging to one of Ed's employers. It was one big, dark, barren room with added kitchen and bathroom appliances. The once-gold carpeting was stained with grease where a former occupant had worked on his motorcycle. I felt like a displaced person but I was so happy to have Ed's loving attention and companionship again that I determined things would get better. We were too poor to go to Esalen anymore but we went to Family Service therapy, both as a couple and individually. Our rented house cost more than the one in Inverness and, when we found we were short on rent money, I tried to get a job as a school psychologist again. The only position available was in Davenport and they wanted someone just starting out, not someone on the brink of retirement. So I got a job as a teacher's aide in Scotts Valley, which suited me much better — shorter hours, no responsibility and a one-semester commitment. I soon learned that in Santa Cruz County almost everyone was overqualified for whatever job they had taken. Before long, I had many friends and activities and after a year of looking we found a home we liked and could afford to mortgage ourselves for. As our income began to increase, we were able to travel. Neither of us was ever sorry that we gave up our demanding jobs and changed our lives.

A Weekend at Esalen

We wound along the Big Sur Coast, its famous scenery shrouded in dark, raggedy clouds and wind blasted rain. Pine, cypress, oak and eucalyptus bowed low over the road, bent down by the relentless storm and adding to out feeling of driving through a tunnel. The windshield wipers clicked crazily, not able to keep the glass clear of the pelting, cascading water. Even the DayGlo green January grass was beaten flat by the pounding rain. The inside of the car windows steamed up faster than I could wipe them clean.

It was 1969 and the two of us were on our way to the country's most famous Center for Personal Growth and Human Potential, hoping to change our lives and save our 26year marriage. Ed had been there before, seeking answers for his own midlife discontents, but it was my first venture into nonconventional therapy and my hopes and expectations were edged and clouded with apprehension.

A modest sign by the highway announced our destination and warned "by reservation only." We turned down a steep road toward the sea and were stopped at a wooden kiosk where a bearded, tie-dyed attendant checked our names on a roster before admitting us. The storm had dwindled to a light patter with erratic gusts, so we were able to look through the trees, across the broad lawns and out to the grey, still angry ocean. Our assigned quarters were like a small motel room from the

OVERCOMING CHILDHOOD ADVANTAGES

fifties, a clean, no frills, make your own bed place. We spoke only of practical matters — where to put things, what to wear, when to go to supper — not of our turbulent feelings. The view from our window was a safe topic and we admired the lovely, rain-drenched plantings, some still blooming in the mild California winter: red geraniums, yellow marguerites, red-hot poker plant, hydrangeas in white, blue and pink, spiky green acanthus and the shiny escalonia hedge, beyond which we could glimpse the wind-piled, churning waves. The eaves dripped steadily and puddles grew on the lawn and in the parking lot.

We joined the supper line at the lodge and marveled at the bountiful heaps of bright garden fresh greens, veggies and fruits. The meal was a choice of chicken curry or brown rice pilaf and was hot, spicy, healthful and delicious. There was home baked bread and crunchy Brown Betty for dessert. We sat on benches at long, rustic tables, shared with people who looked quite different from those seen around our Sacramento home. The general impression was of flowing gowns and robes, sandals, beads, medallions and an abundance of untamed hair on heads and faces. The odor of patchouli oil mingled with the good food smells. There was a lot of hugging and touching as residents of this community greeted each other. But there were also a lot of nervous, expectant "seminarians" like ourselves, trying to blend in and appear relaxed. We spoke with a woman from Germany, a man from Chile, an older couple from Ohio, a young mother from L.A. Five or six different workshops were going on that weekend so there were probably 150 people there. The subjects ranged from Gestalt Psychology with Holy Terror and womanizer Fritz Perls, to massage, Tai Chi, Couples Intensive, Feldenkrais movement and Bioenergetics. We had signed up for the couples one.

Our first meeting was after supper, in another building which looked like a rundown motel but where there was a large carpeted room, empty except for the piles of huge, colorful pillows. We left our shoes at the door, where several pairs were already lined up, and arranged ourselves on the pillows in a large circle. There were about two dozen of us. Our leader was a dark, intense looking man in his forties named Harry, who had given up his career as a dentist to become a therapist. He put us through some exercises which were supposed to break down our reserve and instill trust. We all had to walk around the room in a big circle, making eye contact with everyone we passed and smiling and greeting them. Then we had to pair up with a stranger and sit on the floor, listening to each other take turns telling about ourselves, without any comment other than an encouraging "Yes." Then we were to repeat back all we could remember of what we had heard. I found myself shiftyeyed and embarrassed during these games, afraid I wasn't "doing it right." My classic sweater and skirt outfit seemed as overly proper and stiff as my carefully arranged and sprayed hairdo. But by the time we broke up for the evening, we were all able to hold hands comfortably in the circle. I had never touched a stranger before except for a brief handshake. How doubly strange!

Next morning the storm had gone, leaving the view along the coastline and out to sea achingly clear. It made Cole Weston's photographs look like backdrops for a stage show. We breakfasted on steel cut oatmeal with brown sugar, fresh fruit and blueberry scones. Then an introduction to Tai Chi, on a deck overlooking the ocean with its accompanying roar. I loved the beautiful flowing movements but found them hard to reproduce. In our workshop sessions, I listened and watched, amazed, as people talked about and acted out feelings I had always been taught to think of as bad and best not mentioned. Harry's methods were often confrontational and there were tears, angry yells, pillow pounding, cursing, shaking and sullen silences. I was appalled and frightened, knowing I would never be willing to subject myself to that sort of pain and shame. One woman ran from the room and never returned to the group. But many of these displays ended with embraces and smiles of relief or, at least, an apparent sense of relaxation. How was that possible?

In the evening, Ed coaxed me down to the Baths, where he already felt at home. I was very anxious as I showered my drooping, thrice nursed breasts and protruding belly in the communal shower, and kept my towel tucked carefully around me until the last second before stepping into the tub. Whiffs of marijuana drifted on the sulfury steam and, fortunately for my modesty, the only light was from a few candles. The water was very hot, about 104^0, and I couldn't slip down under as quickly as I would have liked, but gradually I was submerged up to my neck and felt brave enough to look around at my five or six tubmates. There were several tubs in a row on the deck overlooking the ocean, above the crashing surf, and there must have been about twenty people in and out of the tubs or on the massage tables, talking quietly, adding hot or cold water from the hoses, floating silently or playing footsie under the water. Ed was the only man I had ever seen naked and my mother, grandmother, and sister the only women. What an amazing variety of bobbing, floating breasts and penises were on view! Some of the younger men had semi-erections as they nonchalantly climbed right out of the tubs and I saw my first circumcised penis. Fascinating!

The heat began to make me feel lightheaded and I had to slide up to sit on the edge of the concrete tub to cool off. I decided my breasts and belly were of at least average quality in the present company and sat with some confidence. Incense sticks burned in sand-filled saucers around the tubs but there was pot smell, too. A joint was passed and I had a toke, then another when it came around again, then another. My head was swimming and I was still too hot so I climbed out and went to lie down on one of the massage tables, facing the endless sea below and beyond. The full moon was out now and high in the black sky, blotting out the stars around it and sending a golden beam across the water and straight towards me. As I lay looking west beyond the tips of my toes, the huge grey ocean rose right up in a vertical wall and the golden moon sent its broad shining ray directly to me and up my vagina. My fear turned to bliss. When I came back to earth, after some unknown time, Ed was there to help me up the hill and into bed. The next morning was our last session with Harry. He got Ed to do some bioenergetic exercises to "break through his armoring," and had him shaking uncontrollably, roaring with anger and, finally, curled on the carpet like a baby. I was terrified and embarrassed at this loss of dignity but, afterwards Ed seemed beatifically peaceful, Then Harry tried to get me to loosen up and come out of my shell but he finally gave up in disgust, calling me "worse than an impacted wisdom tooth." I was able to enter into the closing exercises, though, which involved lots of hugging, cradling and group lifting. I discovered I really enjoyed being touched and held in this friendly, supportive way. I returned to my ordinary life in Sacramento in a glow of good feeling, but when I tried to pass some of this along by giving my uptight boss a quick hug, he jumped as if I had grabbed his private parts.

 This Esalen experience was the catalyst for me and Ed to make a new beginning. We returned to Esalen many times, both together and separately, and I did learn to come out of my shell — to dance, shake, yell, weep and laugh. Ed retired early from the State bureaucracy and took up blacksmithing. I quit my stressful school job and learned to weave, do Yoga and backpack. We both learned to give each other great massages. Ed gave away his suits and ties and grew a beard. I threw out girdles, nylons, heels and dresses and stopped setting my hair.

We sold our home in the Sacramento suburbs and moved to smaller, simpler quarters in Inverness, then Santa Cruz. We camped and traveled all over Mexico and Hawaii, New Zealand, Nova Scotia, British Columbia, Alaska, and all of our Western States. We created things, he out of iron, me out of yarn; let go of our grown children; played happily with our grandchildren' and sang with the Cabrillo Chorus in Russia. And we both learned to be open with each other, to listen and respect each other, to trust our feelings; we stayed lovingly married for another twenty years, until Ed died.

I still go to Esalen occasionally, and though it has more Yuppies and New Agers than Hippies now and marijuana has been banned, the view is still incredible, the food wonderful, the massages blissful and the Baths healing to body and soul.

Trailer Travels and Travails

The November sun was already dropping below the black silhouette of desert mountains as we crossed the border at the tiny town of San Luis Rio Colorado, south of Yuma. We believed camp spots would be easier to find in Mexico away from the crowded towns of Tijuana, Mexicali or Nogales. Our camping rig consisted of a twelve year old, hard-used brown Ford pickup truck which Ed had gotten cheap at a P.G.&E. auction and an equally venerable fifteen foot trailer we had recently purchased for $1000. It was the only way we could afford to spend a month in Mexico on a single early retirement pension.

As the town of San Luis quickly dwindled to an occasional shack of recycled cardboard and bottles we had the whole empty Sonora desert before us for a free campsite. We felt a real need to stop before dark blotted out our surroundings but there was not even a tree or protective gully in sight. Ed finally selected a lighted, fenced electric transformer station not far from the highway, perhaps believing such an official spot would be a less dangerous place to spend the night than in utter darkness and isolation. I felt exposed, though, in the light from the towers and the humming wires sounded ominous. I thought of all the stories I had heard about Mexican bandits. We fixed the simple supper we had brought and got ready for bed, keeping our light low so we wouldn't attract attention from passing cars — of which there seemed to be almost none. In the night, the

OVERCOMING CHILDHOOD ADVANTAGES

wind blew so hard and so long that I was frightened our trailer would be blown over or the electric wires would come down on us. I slept very little, but the morning finally came, calm and sunny, and I felt ready for more adventure.

That night we spent in Guaymas, in a campground of sorts on the edge of town. The facilities consisted of a leaking toilet and a water faucet which we bypassed in favor of bottled water, but there were shade trees, bright bougainvillea and plenty of company. We watched the brown pelicans competing for leftovers at the fishing dock, then went to a movie at the outdoor theater where we saw a Clint Eastwood western in which his pronouncement of something as "Far out!" was translated in the subtitles as "Fantastico!" We were definitely in another country.

Our plan was to head down the coast as far as Puerto Vallarta, then inland to Guadalajara, San Miguel and Guanajuato, then north to Juarez and El Paso and home to Santa Cruz. I helped drive whenever we weren't in a city but the highway itself was a challenge. It was narrow, with no shoulders and with frequent potholes, rough spots and construction sites which had one-way passage but no flagman. Crawling farm vehicles, dogs, children, goats, pigs or horses could appear suddenly around any bend in the road and buses and trucks roared by us on blind curves, spewing choking fumes. I hadn't been able to master backing the trailer but many of the highway towns we passed through had plenty of pull through spaces for parking at stores and gas stations. Sometimes the Pemex stations would be out of gas if a caravan of R.V.'s had come through and drained them dry.

In downtown Hermosillo, with Ed driving, we had to make a sudden stop in traffic and when we started up again there was a nasty bang and scraping sound from behind the pickup. We had forgotten to fasten the safety chain around the trailer hitch and the trailer had come off! Fortunately, we were on level ground and the Mexicans, instead of honking or yelling at us, got out of their cars and helped us get the truck and trailer reconnected.

The other fastenings we soon learned to check before starting to roll were inside the trailer: the hooks on the cupboard doors and the refrigerator. A couple of sessions of sweeping up broken dishes and wiping cottage cheese or juice off the floor and appliances were all it took to establish a new habit.

We were careful about what we ate and drank, even washing our veggies in iodine water before cooking them, and we were not afflicted with the dread Turista which laid us low on previous trips when we had to eat in restaurants. But we met up with other health hazards. On a very hot, humid night in Topolobampo, surrounded by mangrove swamps, noseeums came right through our screened windows and covered my bare arms, legs and head with bites which burned and itched so badly I could not sleep for several nights. I was still tormented two weeks later whenever I got too warm and wished I could encase myself in an ice pack.

Then, in Guadalajara, where we stayed in a very nice trailer court which allowed some transients like us, we both came down with fever, coughs and aches.

Ed got it first and was so sick I asked the camp manager to send a doctor to check him. This doctor was used to making house calls to Gringo trailers and prescribed antibiotics, but I would have to go to a Farmacia across town to get the medicine. I was daunted by driving that big, old, hard to shift pickup around a big, unknown city at night, knowing only a few words of Spanish. But I made it, even negotiating the hair-raising traffic circles which the Mexicans use as race tracks. Then I got sick, too, and for three or four days we lay miserably around in the cramped, stuffy trailer existing on chicken broth and canned juices.

Finally we recovered enough to make a shaky day trip to Lake Chapala, where we got a traffic ticket for making an illegal U-turn with the trailer. When we objected that we would not be around to appear in court the next week as required, the policeman indicated that he could fix the matter for us with a bit of *mordido*. I think we gave him two dollars extra, the cheapest traffic fine I ever got away with.

In the beautiful colonial town of San Miguel de Allende, we found, on the outskirts, a KOA, filled not with Gringos but with middle class Mexican families on vacation. I didn't care how unethnic the place was, I was very happy to be able to do our laundry, take a shower, and use a toilet which flushed reliably. We walked all over San Miguel, watching expatriate artists, native blacksmiths, religious festivals, and everyday life on the streets.

Our next destination was Guanajuato, a rich silver city in the sixteenth century, now another haven for artists and writers. I was driving across the high plateau on the way there when I saw a group of horseman herding cattle along the wide shoulder of the road on my right. As I passed them, a big bus came hurtling toward me on the left side of the narrow, two lane road and at that instant, a dog following the horseman dashed right in front of the pickup, in pursuit of the bus. There was no way I could stop or swerve to avoid the dog and I felt the truck hit him. Pulling our rig over to the side as soon as possible, I burst into tears, then looked back expecting to se the dog's body and the horseman coming after me to haul me off to jail. Instead, I saw the dog pick himself up from the road and go limping after the men — who did not even look back. That made me cry harder than ever, to think they cared so little about the dog. Ed drove then, dlown into the labyrinthine tunnels of Guanajuato and up into the hills on the far side of town. We were headed for a motel which said it would allow camping vehicles to park in their courtyard and use their bathrooms. The streets of the city are very narrow and steep with sharp turns, dark was coming on fast and we had had a hard day. As Ed tried to turn a tight corner to get up to the motel, the front end of the trailer — which extended out over the back end of the truck in a sort of cabover arrangement — got rammed by an overhanging tree branch. There was a loud crash and tinkle of breaking glass and suddenly the front end of our house on wheels was open to the world. Again, the Mexican bystanders were very helpful — cleaned up the street, guided us up the hill to the motel, and found sheets of cardboard for us to cover up the huge holes in our front end. The motel handyman even helped us hammer the cardboard in place. We were at 6000 feet elevation and it was cold at night but we found a way to make a sort of radiant heater by putting a large ceramic flower pot over a stove burner turned very low.

The next morning we learned there was no place in town to get the trailer fixed and we would have to tow it to Leon about an hour away. We found the repair shop in Leon and the owner agreed to cover the front end of the trailer, where the picture window had been, with plywood. He thought he could get to it that day, if Ed would help him do the work. I wandered around Leon, a busy industrial town that had little interest in tourist attractions, returning to the shop periodically to check on the progress of the repairs, which appeared to me negligible. Finally, Ed was doing almost all the work, paying the shopkeeper for materials and a little advice. I could tell they would not be finished before dark, which was bad because the trailer's brake lights and turn signals had been knocked out by the accident and we would be driving back to Guanajuato with no warning lights on it — illegal even in Mexico and dangerous anywhere. Finally, Ed told me to take the truck and go looking for a motel in Leon which would allow us to park the trailer in their lot overnight while we stayed in one of their rooms. The repair shop owner had already told us there was no place to leave the trailer there overnight. My Berlitz *Spanish for Travelers* had no phrases to cover this situation but I did my best to explain our problem at five or six different motels around town. Assuming they even understood what I wanted, none of them wanted to have a trailer parked in their small parking lots. Feeling discouraged and inadequate, I returned to Ed and found him just finishing up our plywood front end. It was dark and we had at least an hour's drive back to anyplace we could camp but there seemed to be no other choice. Somehow, we made it back to Guanajuato without the trailer being rear ended and without being stopped by the police. This time, we found a camp spot on the outskirts of town so we did not have to take the trailer back through the maze of alleys.

Our time and money were running out so we headed north at last, uphill against a strong headwind through endless miles of high, dry Chilean desert. We would think there was not a single human around, then a lone figure would pop up from nowhere, leading a donkey loaded with scraggly bushes for firewood or hauling jugs of water, In Zacatecas, we treated ourselves to a night in a motel and watched from high up on the hill above the city as the Hall of Records, far below, burned to the ground. The fire had been set by youthful rebels, protesting the latest government's injustices, and the fire trucks had to come from Leon, ninety miles away and uphill all the way.

The last night in Mexico we spent on open land just outside Ciudad Juarez. The hills had been scraped and leveled in preparation for a new housing development, but a few trees had been saved and we found a quiet spot, under a starry sky and undisturbed by bandits or local authorities. The next morning as we drove across the border into El Paso, we both heaved a sigh of relief to be back in the U.S.A., then burst out laughing at the thought of being glad to be in El Paso. That night, in Las Cruces, New Mexico, it snowed and the water inside the trailer froze. It was surely time to get back to Santa Cruz.

During the winter, Ed painstakingly repaired the trailer with glass and aluminum so it looked as good as when we bought it, minus the three foot front overhang. During the next few years, we went on several trips with it around California but never as far as the good 2500 miles we went in Mexico that November. Then the trailer stood in our extra driveway for a few years because we had no vehicle big enough to pull it. It served as a guest room for our grandchildren. Finally, after Ed died, I sold it to a couple who wanted to put it in their yard for their teenage son to live in — to get him out of the house. I actually got teary eyed as they drove it away; there were many wonderful memories within its aluminum walls.

Suburban Crime

Our son, Jonathon, was 18 in 1966 and a sophomore at Berkeley when he introduced us to the evil weed. It was never called marijuana then — just weed, or grass, or pot, or dope. Jonathon came home from college to Sacramento one weekend and we noticed that he would go out for walks around the neighborhood, especially in the evenings — not typical behavior for him. Finally, my husband, Ed, who was more adventuresome and clued in than I and had tried the weed with friends at Esalen, asked Jon if he was smoking on his walks and whether he could get some dope for us. With relief and embarrassment, Jon produced a small baggy of the stuff and papers and showed Ed how to roll his own. I was apprehensive and half believed the tales about this substance being the door to dissolution and donothingness but I tried a couple of tokes when the joint was offered to me. I couldn't feel anything but found the smoke harsh on my throat and strong tasting — indeed, like a weed. I'd been a tobacco smoker for more than twenty years but preferred the mild, menthol cooled brands. However, Ed was experimenting with mid-life changes and was intrigued enough to find us a small supply — not expensive in those days.

That winter, we would often share a joint on Saturday nights and it was not long before I was experiencing amazing streams of colorful images, leading up to fantastic sex. I had a few really otherworldly experiences when stoned, like the time at the Esalen baths when I thought the rays of the full moon were shining across the ocean and penetrating my vagina as I lay naked on a massage table. We never smoked more often than once or twice a week and never tried anything stronger, though Ed read and talked about acid and got some psilocybin buttons. But he lacked the courage to try either substance without a guide and the buttons stayed in the freezer for years until I threw them out when we moved in 1973. By that year, we had decided to leave our stressful, bureaucratic jobs and the allergy-provoking Sacramento Valley and had moved to Inverness to start a simpler life.

It was more difficult to get a supply of weed in a town where we had no friends but, somehow, Ed met another middle-aged man a little younger than himself, who had the proper Connections. I didn't like this man, who called himself "Bear" and managed to be ostentatious in his hippiedom. He had dumped his wife of many years, along with his high paying job, and his present live-in lady, whom he called "Swan," was considerably younger than I was. She wore long, flowing garments of flimsy, Indian bedspread type fabrics and had long, flowing hair which she was always handling, tucking it behind her ears, pulling it into a handful behind her neck or on top of her head, then letting it fall loose again. I couldn't help thinking how it must practically smother Bear during lovemaking, especially if she was on top. Bear and Swan lived in a cabin in Bolinas, a good forty minutes from our small house in Inverness. They invited us to come have supper with them and try out some new dope they had gotten before we bought a lid. I didn't know what to wear; I had happily discarded the pastel pantsuits of my working life when we dropped out and I wore jeans and knit shirts everywhere but I had no flowing garments. I finally settled on a long, flowered skirt, left over from long ago evening parties in Suburbia. I was afraid I still looked more like a school teacher than a Free Soul. We arrived at Bear and Swan's cabin about 6:00 p.m. It was small and too full of old furniture draped with Eastern prints and stuffed with counterculture crafts, symbols, icons and decorations. There were bead curtains to get tangled in, odd shaped pots that held grasses but not water, glass fishing floats, Indian baskets full of sea shells, carvings of whales and woven God's eyes. I could smell incense but no hint of cooking food. We sat on a sagging but colorful couch and were offered acidic red wine and some tasteless dip made from soy beans for our dry rye husks. Swan didn't say much but Bear made up for that by relating his many fantastic adventures all over the world.

What we had come to buy was finally brought forth, two joints rolled and passed. I could tell at the first toke that this was stronger stuff than I had had before. We hadn't done pot as much since quitting work and when we did I noticed it was drying my throat painfully and making my stomach hurt so the discomfort interfered with my pleasure. This stuff that Bear had for us made my head swim and my empty stomach cringe. After two tokes I stopped inhaling and just passed it along. But Ed and Bear seemed to be engaged in some sort of contest as to who could smoke the most. Finally, when I thought I was well started on a stomach ulcer from hunger and smoke irritation, Swan brought out some kind of cold food. It might have been tabouli salad; I know it was unappetizing and hard to digest but we forced ourselves to eat a little. Ed had only a few bites before he staggered up out of his chair, saying he was going to be sick, and just made it to the bathroom. He came out looking very grey and shaky and sweating heavily, saying he needed to go home. There were expressions of concern, apologies and hurried good-byes while I got our coats and we all helped Ed out to the car. He could barely walk and vomited again on their front walk. Terribly embarrassed, I got him in the car and headed back along the winding road to Inverness. I had to stop twice so Ed could throw up again, into the eucalyptus leaves along the side of the road. He slept until almost noon the next day and told me later he thought he was dying the night before. We didn't see Bear or Swan again and didn't smoke for quite a long time after that. We hadn't bought any of Bear's supply and Ed started experimenting with marijuana brownies, using small amounts he got from Jonathon. He seemed to enjoy them but I never felt any effect from them. Before long we moved to Santa Cruz, then Aptos, where we had our own house and a large, secluded yard. Weed had gotten a lot more expensive by the late 70's and its cultivation a lot more sophisticated. Ed got several books from the library on growing the weed, particularly sinsemilla, and with seed obtained from some one of our children he planted two five gallon cans and placed them in a hidden corner of our backyard, invisible from any passing car or person. He tended his plants tenderly, drying his crop in our attic and using most of it in brownies which still gave me no charge. Ed had been diagnosed with glaucoma and was convinced from his reading that pot would alleviate or control his eye problem. He was on his third crop and ready to harvest it when we returned from a weekend away and found the plants had been stolen from their hiding place. We had forgotten that the meter readers and maybe some stray yard boy or roaming teenager would have spotted their lush greenery. Ed gave up on growing the stuff then and restricted his use to an occasional pipeful of hash from one of our children or their spouses. I found this form of pot too strong for me and pretty much gave it up completely except for a toke or two when a smoke was passed at gatherings of friends or relatives. I was smoking tobacco which was much worse for my health, and Ed's. Years later, after Ed died and I was having a lot of pain from arthritis, my son-in-law suggested that a little hash might alleviate the pain and presented me with a small amount and a tiny pipe. I kept that possible relief hidden away in the antique slant top desk from my childhood for at least a year without the urge to use it. Finally, I gave it away to a young man who was staying with me for a couple of months while recovering from a broken marriage and a lost job. He seemed to need it more than I did. My drug of choice became one beer before supper but lately I have switched to cranberry juice.

AT THE BOTTOM OF THE GRAND CANYON

It is our last night on the Colorado and we are camped on a sandbar 220 miles downstream from Lee's Ferry where our rafts put in twelve days ago. There are three rafts for the fourteen adventurers and a fourth to carry food and gear. Gary, Bert, Ginger and Christa are the expert oars person guides who have brought us here. Our group includes a geologist from Texas, a mechanical engineer from Phoenix, an ex Secret Service man from Utah, a Swiss woman from Boston, an Australian woman photographing the trip for a travel magazine there, four young Frenchmen and a middle-aged couple from Salt Lake City who smoke too much. My husband, Ed, and I are the oldest by at least twenty years.

By now, we feel like old pros at riverbank camping. We help haul the rafts up onto the sandbar where the guides secure them to branches or rocks. We form a brigade to pass all the waterproof bags full of our gear up onto higher ground and all the food and cooking equipment to the spot the guides have designated as tonight's kitchen. Then we each drag our heavy rubber bags up the sandbank, floundering in the sliding grains, and to find a flat spot to pitch our tent, not too close to the next one. We tried sleeping without a tent but surprise showers in the middle of the night have made us cautious.

One of our guides hauls up the big bucket which is our potty and designates the spot for it; with luck, there is some sparse vegetation to give an illusion of privacy. The bucket is only for solid waste, all of which must be taken out of the Canyon with us. Peeing is done in the river, to keep the few small, heavily used campsites from getting smelly. Fifteen thousand people come down this stretch of the Colorado every summer, yet it seems clean and litter free, the millions of gallons of rushing water washing away the traces of human presence. After so many days, we have all become very nonchalant about peeing in the presence of others, merely turning our backs or squatting at the edge of the water. The oarswomen are adept at slipping into the river as we float downstream, hanging off a locked oar and relieving their bladders before flipping back on board. (Of course, it's much easier for the men.) Our drinking and cooking water comes from the river, too, but it is filtered before use — and most people considerately pee downstream from where our water is drawn.

The Park Service regulates our cooking arrangements, too. No gathering or burning of wood is allowed so the boat crew uses a propane stove, and, for baking, charcoal briquettes on top of as well as under a heavy Dutch oven. All ashes must be hauled out of the Canyon. We are served wonderful hot breads and even delicious cake baked in the Dutch Oven. All the food is great because the cargo boat carries huge ice chests with dry ice in the bottoms, so we have fresh fruits, vegetables and meats every day. Cans of beer and pop are tied up in net bags and towed behind the rafts so there is always a cold drink available during the hot afternoons. It is the first week in September and the sun is still strong, though when it is hidden by clouds or high cliffs we can soon feel the chill in the air. The river water is 51^0 so our evening baths are hasty. Bedtime is early because it gets dark about seven thirty and we are allowed only one propane lantern for the whole group and that to be used only in emergencies. I read by flashlight in my sleeping bag but not for long. We are up at 6:00 and on the river by 8:00.

The only beaches large enough to accommodate our group of eighteen are usually where side canyons enter the Colorado. Big boulders spill from these canyons during flash floods and form a rock and gravel bar which keeps the sand from being washed away. Tonight, a few tamarisk trees provide us with a little shade and privacy. The river rushing sounds like a continuous, gentle surf and on the far side the red cliffs go straight up nine hundred feet. We have rowed and floated past more than a dozen distinct rock layers which emerged as the river cut deeper into the Canyon: first the almost black, 1.7 billion year old Vishnu schist, then pink and red Zoroaster granite, redwall limestone, light grey Chinle shale, red hermit shale, buff colored Coconino sandstone and last, the cream colored top layer of Kaibab limestone, 66 million years young. Gary tells us how each later was formed as we go; it is the first time I have found geology exciting.

Along the river we have seen bighorn sheep and muledeer and wild burros taking a drink, teals and mergansers bobbing in the shallows, hawks, ravens and turkey vultures soaring overhead, ground squirrels scampering over the rocks and coyotes slipping between them, scorpions, millipedes, bluetailed skinks and desert mice in our campgrounds and swooping bats every evening. We have listened to the clear, descending liquid warble of the canyon wren, and watched two peregrine falcons catching, tearing apart and devouring a kestrel on the cliff across from our tent site.

In the last 12 days we have screamed our way through more than one hundred serious rapids with names like Sockdolager, Upset, Surprise, Sheer Wall, Fishtail, Rancid Tuna and Nankoweap. Our rafts have been tipped, tossed, spun and slapped, plowing through the middle of up to fifteen foot waves and saturating us with cold spray. I have not felt this sort of terror and excitement since my first teenage roller coaster ride. Our

OVERCOMING CHILDHOOD ADVANTAGES

oarspeople are strong, experienced and skillful but they have to steer 22 foot rubber rafts, loaded with people and gear, using 14 foot oars, through the huge waves and around rocks, eddies and sinkholes with the water rushing at thousands of cubic feet per second, over drops of up to ten vertical feet. Whenever there is a really tough rapid we pull into shore and the boat people scout the situation, deciding which side of which rocks would be the least risky route. Since the water level fluctuates greatly, due to the variations in the amount released upstream at the Glen Canyon Dam, every day and time of day can present a different set of conditions. At Crystal Rapids, where giant boulders have tumbled into the river blocking it halfway across, the route was deemed too dangerous for passengers to ride through. Luckily, we were able to walk around, rock hopping across the boulders for half a mile while we watched our lightened craft spinning and bouncing between the rocks as our rowers battled the current. All four of our boats made it but some other parties opted to portage their craft across the rocks.

There were calm, peaceful stretches between the rapids when the canyon opened out, the river widened and moved lazily and we were presented with long vistas of towering cliffs, peaks and mesas. I had visited the Grand Canyon from above a number of times, both North and South Rims, but I did not fully appreciate the grandeur and immensity of it until I viewed it from the bottom. In the quiet times between rapids we could doze and dream in the sun or take a turn at the oars if we wanted exercise. If the wind came blowing up the Canyon, these flat stretches were a tedious challenge to keep the rafts moving downstream rather than rowing in place.

Not all our time was spent on the river. Every day we came ashore at least once, to eat our picnic lunch and explore side canyons with names like Saddle Canyon, Deer Creek, Stone Creek, Elves' Chasm, Havasu and Bright Angel. Many of these canyons presented us with steep, challenging hikes lasting several hours. First, a scramble up several hundred feet of red rock, with an occasional boost from below or pull from above for those of us with shorter legs or less agility. Then walking along narrow ledges on the brink of deep, water carved canyons and hauling ourselves over rocks and across streams. But we were always rewarded with lovely waterfalls and cascades, lush hanging valleys, turquoise pools with travertine terraces, groves of mesquite and cottonwood tangled with grape vines, delicate wild flowers and thick green moss and maidenhair ferns growing ten feet from prickly pear cactus. We saw water ouzels dipping for insects, blue darning needles, orange dragonflies, black and yellow swallowtails, lavender morning glories and many of the big white trumpets of sacred Datura. In some places we found Anasazi pictographs and the remains of their granaries.

On our next to last day we have to run the biggest rapid of all at Lava Falls, a 37 foot drop with a difficulty rating of 10, the highest. Bert, our boatman, scouted it carefully and headed out, standing up and rowing hard. Christa was with us, in the back of the boat. We made sure our life jackets were snug, got a good grip on the rope around the edge of the raft and braced ourselves. When we hit the bottom of the trough after the first big wave, I somehow lost hold with my weaker left hand and got flipped out over the side. Scott, the man from Salt Lake, was also flipped out over the side. Ed, who was up front, said the wave was fifteen feet from trough to crest, very steep and sharp. The boat went through the top five feet of this wave, which was a mixture of air and water, then crashed back down onto the surface of the river. Bert lost one of the oars, Scott disappeared under the raft but I never lost hold with my right hand, and rode on down through the next four waves, enjoying the sensation of being in the boiling water. Scott reappeared on the far side of the boat, much to everyone's relief, Bert grabbed the spare oar and retrieved the one that had escaped downstream and Christa somehow managed to haul all 150 pounds of me straight up over the side of the boat and back in, Bert did the same for Scott. My straw hat, tied firmly under my chin, stayed in place the whole time. Bert rowed us ashore at a handily located beach and we had a fine lunch with beer and lots of fussing over us while we dried out. Tonight we are having a last night celebration, complete with chilled wine, grilled steaks, roasted potatoes and corn, green salad and cake. Everyone is dressed up in some way with bright bandanas, muumuus, beads, a skirt or toga, fashioned from a sleeping bag liner, even a necktie that someone brought We all take pictures and retell the stories of the adventures we have shared. Beneath the camaraderie we are already thinking of that hot shower and soft bed and comfortable chair we will find tomorrow night.

Back in our atrocious Las Vegas hotel casino the next night, clean, anointed with lotions, fed and rested, we take stock of our adventure. These were the casualties: Two pairs of broken sunglasses One lost water bottle One lost pair of rain pants One discarded pair of worn out tennis shoes Fine sand in everything we took, including my camera Dry, sore, cracked skin Huge, dark bruises on my upper arms from falling out and being hauled back into the boat Scrapes and cuts slow to heal because of being wet so long Aching joints from cold water, overuse and lack of comfortable places to rest

This was what made it all worthwhile:

The most awesome, fascinating, beautiful, exciting, unforgettable experience of our lives. How many grandmothers can brag that they got flipped out going over Lava Falls?!

DO IT YOURSELF
VISION QUEXT

It was my second solo backpacking trip and the first on which I was completely away from familiar territory or other hikers. I was 52 years old, 20 pounds overweight and had been a smoker for more than 30 years. But I had gotten hooked on backpacking when I was 50, after years of inactivity and had been preparing myself with lengthy hikes and overnights with friends or with the Sierra Club. I was eager to test my newly developed skills and courage. I chose an area just south of the Yosemite Park border and west of the Minarets summit in the Sierra. It was beautiful, about 7000 to 8000 feet in elevation (my favorite scenery) and not heavily used. It took me most of a day to drive there in my old Ford van from my home near Santa Cruz, so I spent that night parked in an informal camp area with a few other hikers and fisher people. There were warnings posted about bears, ordering campers to keep their ice chests in their car trunks. Vans don't have trunks and mine was a window van so I hid my food under a blanket and drew all the curtains, but I had to leave one window open a couple of inches because it was roasting hot. All night I imagined a huge, hairy paw reaching in that window and grabbing my ice chest — or me. But I had no intruders and the morning was beautiful so I got an early start. This was not a popular trail and I met few fellow travelers. I made slow but steady progress and by mid afternoon was up around 9000 feet with gorgeous views of the Sierra Crest to the east. I passed a

OVERCOMING CHILDHOOD ADVANTAGES

couple of fishermen and then found I had to cross a fast cascading stream. My balance was poor and I knew I couldn't cross by walking on the rocks and logs which had been placed right where the stream plunged over the edge of a perilous vertical drop. So, after looking around to be sure the fishermen weren't close enough to witness my shame, I took off my jeans and boots, stuffed them in my pack, and sat down, straddling the log. I pushed my pack in front of me across the log, inching my bottom along behind it.

It was scary and the water was icy cold on my legs but I made it to the other side without getting anything very wet except my underpants — which dried quickly in the mountain air.

When I had reassembled myself, I decided it was time to look for a good campsite. There was plenty of water nearby and nothing but privacy — not a soul to be seen. I found a nice, flat spot for my tent, with spectacular views of the Minarets and set about making camp. I hadn't been backpacking long enough to invest in good equipment so my tent was a flimsy, sagging $20 number from KMart, with no rain fly. But I got it pitched and made my unappetizing freeze dried meal, then tried to find a place to hang the rest of my food out of the reach of bears. I was up almost to tree line so the tallest trees were about 8 feet high and about as big around as my leg. But I hung my supplies as high as I could reach, then crawled into my tent to read by flashlight. It was too cold to sit outside and no fires were allowed. During the night, I dozed intermittently, my ears sharp for animal noises. I had a magical belief that one layer of orange ripstop nylon would protect me from raccoons, bobcats, snakes, skunks and even bears! Sometime in the middle of that long, cold, uncomfortable, lonely night I was sure I heard a bear going after my food stash. I had my spoon and pan ready and made a great banging and yelling until everything was quiet outside. I was afraid to unzip the tent and take a look.

After that, I lay there for a long time trying to relax and get warm. Sometime during that meditation I came to an acceptance of the fact that I was going to die — someday if not now — and that that would be O.K. whenever it happened. The sunrise over the Minarets was glorious and I felt calm and proud of myself. When I got back to my car that afternoon, I had not seen another person for 24 hours. Some folks spend hundreds of dollars to be put through the kind of experience I had by an Outdoor Adventure group. I continued backpacking for almost 15 years but undertook only one other solo trip — and I aborted that one by hiking back to my car in the twilight because I was so lonely and uncomfortable. After all, I had already proved I could do it.

Ed's solution to backpacking.

OVERCOMING CHILDHOOD ADVANTAGES

GETTING TO ALASKA

I spent months in preparation reading John McPhee's *Coming into the Country*, studying the *Lonely Planet Travel Survival Kit*, tour company literature and magazine articles, poring over maps and subscribing to Milepost, the mile by mile description of the Alcan Highway, from Dawson Creek through Whitehorse and all the way to Fairbanks. My plan was to drive from Aptos to Prince Rupert, British Columbia, take the Alaska ferry to Skagway, drive over Chilkoot Pass to Whitehorse where I would join the Alcan, then on to Tok, Fairbanks, Denali, Anchorage and the Kenai Peninsula, camping all the way and doing lots of hiking. Then drive home all the way via the Alcan. I waited until July so there wouldn't be snow on the roads and planned to be gone about six weeks.

Ed refused to go with me — too much driving and camping for his taste — but he did everything he could to prepare my '72 orange VW poptop for the journey. He mounted the spare tire on the front and a spare spare on the roof. He bought a tire pump that would run off the cigarette lighter and gunk to squirt in a flat tire to make it last till you could change it. He drilled me on changing the tires and provided me with a special tool he made to help me loosen and tighten the lug nuts. He created heavy screen covers for the headlights and a removable one for the windshield as protection against the flying gravel of the Alcan. He bought extra fuses for the electrical connections, an extra fan belt, and spare parts and fluids for everything I might need which I could handle myself.

I had camped by myself around the western states for as long as five weeks and two years earlier I had spent almost three weeks camping and hiking alone in British Columbia and Alberta, so I felt confident in my ability to do this trip. My friends all thought I was very brave and/or crazy.

My first night out I spent with friends, near Arcata, but then I was on my own, heading for the Oregon Coast. Getting hypnotized by highway driving was a problem for me but I had bought a negative ionizer which was supposed to help me stay alert and I used a lot of tea, Pepsi, cigarettes, snacks, taped music, and cool air blowing in my face to keep me from falling asleep at the wheel. I didn't try to drive more than about 300 miles a day but still my back got to aching. I was 60 years old in 1983, and my bones and muscles were getting tired.

I took three nights to get through Oregon and Washington, reveling in the natural beauty around me, finding lovely campsites along the way and arriving early enough in the afternoons to explore the areas on foot. I was still riding the wave of my departure adrenaline, in spite of having to cope with rain, narrow roads, logging trucks and tourist traffic, ranging from bicyclists to gigantic Winnebagos. Rounding a tight curve near Reedsport, in a long procession of vehicles, I came upon a little fawn at the side of the road, its broken leg dangling, the bone protruding, its mother trying to nudge it up the bank away from traffic. I knew it didn't have a chance of surviving and that none of us travelers could help it and my eyes blurred with tears.

In the evenings, I chased away loneliness for an hour by going to Park Ranger talks which, even when boring, always featured a cheerful, leaping fire, a nice slide show and some contact with other people. Couples sometimes asked me, "Aren't you afraid, traveling all alone?" And I began to wonder if I should be.

Arriving at the border of British Columbia, near the tiny town of Sumas, I did not feel welcomed into Canada, I had waited in line behind an RV towing a boat on a trailer which got pulled over because of some suspicious looking water weeds hanging from the boat's propeller. The border guards seemed suspicious of me, too: an old woman, traveling alone for pleasure? They searched my camper, briefly, asked if it were in good condition (it was 11 years old but I still thought of it as "new." Our other car was a '61 VW beetle), wanted to know bow much money I had with me and how long I was planning to stay in their country, and asked me if I was carrying a firearm, Mace, liquor, cigarettes or fruit. I felt insulted, after all my careful preparations for the trip.

That night I camped at the KOA in Hope, a small town surrounded by spectacular mountains and the rushing, murky grey Fraser River. I changed money, did laundry, showered, and bought groceries at the Overwaitea Market, a name I thought appropriate for my body shape at that time. Now I was ready to tackle the North Country. It was a nice enough campground but the mosquitoes were ferocious, biting me through 2 layers of cloth, and there were evil looking black slugs on the paths as I walked around the grounds. The weather was cloudy and gloomy most of the day and my stomach was acting up, maybe from the anxiety I felt crossing into a "foreign country", even one so much like our own. Reading, writing, walking, music and crosswords helped fill up the long, lonely evening but my dreams were of danger and violence.

Heading north the next day, I found Canadian scenery as spectacular as I remembered it: rushing, glaciered rivers, steep, craggy snow patched mountains, forests and meadows in soft shades of grey, green, tan and rose, highlighted by the starker blacks and whites above. About halfway along the Cariboo Highway to Prince George, I found another lovely campground, amongst firs, at long, skinny Lac La Hache. Provincial Parks in British Columbia provide free firewood, cut to convenient lengths, and as evening came on, with no Ranger talk for entertainment, I decided to build my first campfire. I had brought a hatchet but splitting kindling was not something I had done; Ed always built our fires. I stood a log on end and delivered a sharp blow with the hatchet, but neglected to remove quickly enough the hand holding the log and chopped off a bit of finger tip. It was not a serious injury but it was bloody and painful and interfered with my already minimal manual dexterity for several days. Mostly, I felt very dumb. That night I slept poorly and woke up feeling discouraged and anxious, the feelings manifesting themselves in weird chest pains. Probably heartburn, I told myself, but it was still scarry. It was so cold at night that I bought a pair of long johns at the Prince George Sears before I headed west, feeling very far from home. The highway was hemmed in by mile after mile of tall skinny fir trees so it was like driving through a long, green tunnel. There were no billboards (a blessing except when one is looking for some sign of human presence), no buses, very few trucks and only one Royal Canadian Mounted Police car in 200 miles. I saw "Watch Out for Moose" signs but the only wild animal visible was a coyote crossing the road. Occasionally, there was a farmhouse in a clearing with a line of washing hanging out in the rain. When I did come out of the woods, there were grand views of enormous snowy mountains in three directions. Why did I need company?

 At nightfall, in a tiny, wet, almost deserted campground I watched a motor home owner pull in, get out and chop wood, light the ritual fire and get back inside, leaving the fire to burn all by itself. Once he came out, put another log on, then returned to his wife and dinner inside. Later, I was ashamed of my scornfullness because this couple invited me over to share the warmth of their still burning fire after supper, then when the rain began again, they invited me inside for the evening. I had been having chest pains and heebie-jeebies and badly needed company, so I was happy to chat about traveling, retirement, kids, and grand kids.

By the next night, I was in Terrace, only 95 miles from Prince Rupert where I had a reservation on the Alaskan Ferry. I had been driving through gorgeous, wild country, mostly unpopulated except for a few Indian bungalows, Shocking pink fireweed and fields of white daisies lined the road and the mountains never stopped. I visited Ksan Indian village, watched Indians spearing fish at a fish ladder on the Skeena River and saw twin falls emerging from a glacier. After driving and sightseeing all day in the rain, I treated myself to a motel with kitchenette for $29. I was getting cabin camper fever and the upsetting physical symptoms weren't helping any. The night before I had imagined the camper was my coffin and wondered, if I died in my sleep, how long it would take for someone to find me. The first thing I did when I got in the motel was turn on the TV so I could hear a human voice.

The 95 miles to Prince Rupert the next morning were terrifying. I knew in my head there was nothing wrong with my heart but I could not seem to break out of the trap of anxiety — pain — more anxiety and feelings of being dizzy and disconnected. I drove those last miles by hanging onto the steering wheel with rigid, numb determination, as if I were in a raft on a wild river where I could be swept off course and crash at any moment. I had driven more than 2000 miles alone but I was too scared to imagine myself driving several thousand more, no matter how marvelous the sights along the way. I felt ashamed and defeated but I knew I had to give up. Was it the dying fawn, the border guards, the black slugs, the cut finger, the bad dreams, the persistent rain and cold or just the snowballing loneliness?

The municipal campground in Prince Rupert — the only camping facility anywhere around — was a crowded, dirty, miserable place. It was really just an end of the road parking lot and waiting room for ferry passengers. The city didn't turn anyone away, so all 150 campsites were filled plus vehicles parked side by side and end to end in the grassy spots between. The toilets and trash cans were overflowing and the view was of the chain link fence, the highway and another parking lot of 100 or so cars and RV's left in storage by people who went on the ferries without them. But I found a spot and went to call Ed, to tell him I was giving up and heading home. I felt like a stupid, neurotic chicken and when I heard his voice, I could barely speak through my tears. But, Oh, Frabjous Day! He said he would come to rescue me! He'd fly to Prince Rupert in a couple of days, we'd go on to Juneau and Glacier Bay on the ferries, then bring the camper back home by ferry to Vancouver Island and south. I was elated, thrilled, grateful and my chest pains and dizziness vanished. My humbling experience had taught me something very important about recognizing my limitations and listening to my body.

We did have wonderful adventures in Juneau and Glacier Bay. Driving back along Vancouver Island, the camper sustained the only damage of the entire trip. A big truck driving in front of us on the paved road threw some loose gravel at the camper windshield and cracked it. Of course, since we weren't on the Alcan Highway, we didn't have the screen Ed made on the windshield.

The next summer, a woman friend and I flew to Anchorage and rented a camper. We spent five days exploring Denali National Park and five days on the Kenai Peninsula, including a boat trip to Kenai Fjords. It was all glorious and expensive and I've been wanting to go back ever since.

Encounter at the Border

The road from Arusha to the Kenyan border was mostly straight and paved. Nasser, our Tanzanian driver, made our seven passenger Nissan Van hurtle along it at speeds up to 70 miles an hour, slaloming around the deep potholes and slowing only for breaks in the pavement, muddy ruts, stalled trucks or herds of goats and cattle crossing in front of us. The rain greened savanna, dotted with whistling thorn bushes and umbrella acacias, rolled out on either side of the road to dark volcanic peaks in the distance. We had left behind, in wilder places, the zebras, elephants, wildebeests, giraffes, impalas, lions, cheetahs, hyenas, buffalo, wart hogs, hippos, rhinos, baboons and other safari creatures but occasionally we could see a herd of gazelles. This was Maasai country and we passed some of them walking along the road in their bright red shawls, always with a stick in hand for "protection" against wild beasts, we were told. A few were riding bicycles or thumbing rides and begging, one with a large cowboy hat topping his traditional outfit.

Nasser was in a hurry because he had another group of safarians to pick up after he delivered us, or maybe he had gone speed crazy after our two weeks of inching, jolting, bouncing, sluing, wheel spinning, bone jarring, waiting to be towed again experiences on impassable back roads. Two hours of speeding brought us to Natanga, the congested scruffy-looking border town where we went through Customs, drove through the open iron gate into Kenya, and found that our Kenyan driver and van, to take us to Nairobi, had not arrived yet. It was 10:00 A.M. and there was no place to go and nothing to do while we waited. Nasser found a tiny spot of shade to park in and one of our group checked out the restroom facilities in the nearby Dream Restaurant but brought back a report which discouraged any of the rest of us from using them. My fellow travelers sat in the van, writing in their journals, going over bird lists, reading or doing crossword puzzles but I was itching to get out and wander a little with my camera.

 I started to take a picture of the Kenyan and Tanzanian flags flying above the guard tower at the border but our guide warned me that to do so was against the law, so I turned my camera eye to the rutted street and the little shops lining it. Huge trucks, buses and heavy equipment clogged the town on both sides, many of the vehicles seemingly abandoned but presumably waiting for their drivers to complete official paper work or have a beer. The rows of small shops were advertising everything from hardware and hotdogs to Fax service and investments. In the U.S. these shacks would have been razed for urban renewal. A few chickens and goats wandered free, men pushed wheelbarrows filled with plastic water barrels or building material, women in beautiful fabrics artfully draped about their shoulders, hips and waists, walked past with huge bags of grain or baskets of goods balanced on their heads. I wanted to take their pictures but was not willing to be that intrusive. A few children came up to me, wanting money in exchange for my taking their pictures, but I knew if I gave out any coins I would immediately be surrounded by a dozen more beggars and unshakable vendors of ugly tourist souvenirs I did not want.

 Then a tall young man approached me. He was handsome, with very dark skin and a bright, white smile.

 "Will you take my picture?" He asked in clearly spoken

English, "in front of my store?" He indicated the small hole in the wall grocery we were standing near.

"I don't want to pay," I hedged. "I have no Kenyan shillings."

"Not for money," he said. "Just send me the picture."

I asked him how he learned such good English.

"I have been through the Fourth Form of Secondary School," he declared proudly. Then, ruefully, "I couldn't finish, though, because there was not enough money. I must work in my father's store."

I decided it would be all right to take his picture and walked with him over to his shop, keeping an eye on my safari van so the rest of my group would see where I was. I took one picture of him in the doorway and one with him inside, leaning across the front counter. Canned goods, bottled water and household supplies were piled on the shelves.

He told me his name was Elvis Ngigi Mathu and that he was 22 years old, the son of a Maasai mother and Kikuyu father.

"My father has another wife, a Kikuyu wife, and 11 children. I am the oldest. He owns this store but there are too many children and not enough money to give them an education. I went to Maasai primary school, then to secondary school in a town down the road but the others will not get to go there. My father made a mistake, having so many children. We will not be able to leave here."

I asked Elvis if he was married and he said, "No, I do not have any wealth to offer a bride. But I will not have more than one wife. My father must work very hard in this store."

"Maybe he will be able to retire someday", I said from my naive American perspective.

"The government retirement pensions are so small that no one can live on them", Elvis replied. "People must work until they are too old to do so."

I tsktsked and asked about the scholarships to University. Surely, Elvis should be going there. He smiled in a sweetly forlorn way and told me scholarships are very hard to get. "One hundred applicants for every one," he declared and went on to bemoan his government's "rich men" who spend money on themselves rather that on the schools, pensions, roads and health care the country needs. It sounded strangely familiar and unlikely to change under the present entrenched authoritarian leader.

"You are retired?" Elvis asked me. I told him I was and he said "What do you do with your time, then"

"I travel, take pictures, write, sing in a chorus, visit my children and grandchildren, read, do things for my church, walk on the beach and in the mountains, listen to music," I confessed, feeling more and more guilty as I listed my pleasures, few of which will likely ever be his. "Someday maybe you can do these things," I couldn't stop myself from saying. He smiled at me gently, not even bothering to contradict me.

"It is very boring working here," he said then and it was true. Not a single customer had come along while we talked. "I read books by Danielle Steele — for my adventure and escape. Do you know that author?"

"Yes," I said, "but I haven't read any of her books."

"What do you like to read?" I told him I was just then reading *Out of Africa* and tried to explain what it was about but he had not heard of it or of Dinesen.

Then Elvis asked a question I could not understand. I had to ask him to repeat the words three times. It sounded like "uddcakes." Finally, I grasped that he wanted to know about earthquakes in California and what it was like to live with them.

"They can be very frightening," I told him. "But I grew up with them and you get used to them — the way you are used to your life here." He nodded.

It was time for me to return to my van, continue my journey

back to Nairobi, London and California. Elvis and I exchanged addresses and I promised to send his pictures. "When is your birthday?" he asked. I told him and he said, shyly, "Perhaps I will send you a birthday card."

"If you do, I will write to you." I promised.

As I was leaving, Elvis' father came in to relieve him in the store. Elvis had told me this man was 55, but he looked 75. I suppose Elvis may look like that in 30 years.

I returned to my tour group feeling helpless and a little ashamed as I often do with people less fortunate than I. It was easier to think about all the wonderful, exciting wild animals I had seen. I didn't have to feel guilty for not helping them; they all seemed quite happy with their lives.

Elvis did send me a birthday card and we exchanged a few letters in the next two years. His were full of his desire to escape from his present life and his feelings of being helplessly stuck in it. Finally, he asked me if I would sponsor his coming to the U.S. but I had to tell him I couldn't do that. His last letter was more cheerful. He had managed to save $80, the train fare to Nairobi, and was sure of getting a job there and leaving Natanga behind.

Singing for the Soviets

My husband, Ed, and I spent many years singing in the Cabrillo College Chorus when we lived in Aptos, near Santa Cruz. The Chorus was our main musical and recreational activity for more than fifteen years. Our leader and conductor for much of that time was Anthony (Tony) Antolini, a gifted professor of Music and Slavic Languages at the Community College. Tony built the group up from a lackluster bunch of 20 or 30 to a force of 80 or more enthusiastic and dedicated singers. He instituted auditions but relied more on the applicant's ability to accurately reproduce pitch and rhythm than at skill in sightreading. His choices of unusual and beautiful music attracted some outstanding singers who helped to raise the performance standards of the whole group.

The Chorus got so professional sounding under Tony's guidance and coaching that we had a yearly date to sing with the Santa Cruz County Symphony in its final concert every May. We did *Carmina Burana,* Bernstein's *Chichester Psalms,* Mozart's *Mass in C* and *Requiem,* Brahms' *German Requiem,* the sacred music of Faure, Poulenc, Durufle, Verdi and many other greats. We were good, even music critics of the big city newspapers said so! I'm not at all religious but that kind of music is tremendously moving to me.

Tony had something even more in mind for us. He had spent a year at Moscow University, finishing his doctorate in Slavic Languages. He had discovered that the manuscript for

Rachmaninoff's *Liturgy of Saint John Chrysostom* had been lost when sacred music was banned in the 1917 Revolution, but had recently been discovered in an isolated Russian Orthodox monastery in the wilds of Upstate New York. Tony went to track it down but found that it existed only in part books, that is separate scores for Soprano, Alto, Tenor and Bass. He spent all summer combining the parts into one score that would be readable by an amateur American choir like us. He found a conductor's score on micro film in the Library of Congress. Then he transliterated all the Russian words into pronounceable syllables and translated it into English. He had already taught us a piece from Rachmaninoff's *Vespers,* which we had performed to everyone's delight and listener's praise.

So, when college started up again in the fall of 1985, the chorus began studying Russian and the tricky rhythms and intervals of Rachmaninoff. It was hard work but we loved the music and were willing to work hard. Singers came from Monterey, San Francisco, even Los Banos, just to sing with us on Tuesday nights. There were sectionals held at the homes of people who had pianos and confident voices.

We couldn't concentrate completely on the Rachmaninoff *Liturgy* that Fall until after our three Christmas concerts which were a big Santa Cruz tradition. Our audiences numbered 500 people a night for three nights running at the Holy Cross Church downtown. But by Spring, with continuing hard work, we were ready to do some local concerts of the Liturgy and charge admission. We performed the one hour, 20 movement *Liturgy* at Holy Cross in Santa Cruz, the Carmel Mission, the San Jose Performing Arts Theater, San Francisco's Grace Cathedral and other Bay Area concert halls. We were seeking publicity and money for our big trip to the then USSR. Tony's connections in Moscow had led to our being the first American choir invited to sing in the Soviet Union since the

Revolution of 1917 and the first to perform Rachmaninoff's Liturgy, which had been buried/lost for 70 years. The trip would cost us $2000 apiece for our transportation and hotels only, and many of the students and struggling musicians could not afford that, so we had created a scholarship fund with our concert earnings. Singers and fellow travelers kept signing up to go as well as significant others and Russia-lovers We called the nonsingers "groupies"

In the summer of 1986 we had a concert tour of the East Coast of the U.S. where we performed the *Liturgy* and some American Spirituals for crowds in the Washington Cathedral, St. John the Divine in New York City, Boston Cathedral and in Tony's home town of Thomaston, Maine, where we also sang selections with the choir of his Episcopal Church. We made a lot more money for scholarships and tour expenses and, in the fall, when college started up again, more singers enrolled so we had a chorus of nearly 150 plus all the relatives and Groupies who wanted to go to Russia with us.

We kept polishing the *Liturgy* in our fall rehearsals, while also learning and performing our Christmas concerts repertoire. I had to take a couple of weeks off after an unexpected mastectomy on Oct. 27 but I was determined to go on the tour so I recovered fast though it was a couple of months before I could hold up my heavy music in my left arm without additional support from my right hand. I was very lucky not to need radiation or chemo, so I was on that plane with the others two days after Christmas, 1986.

We were a real mix of singers and fellow travelers from 18 year old students to grandparents in their 70's and from old hippy types to doctors, attorneys and business people, but we were all dedicated to performing this beautiful music and making this a peace and friendship mission to the Soviets.

Gorbachev, Glasnost and perestroika were now the temper

of the times and we were warmly welcomed and lavishly praised everywhere we went. We flew to Helsinki, over the pole, then took the train to Leningrad (St. Petersburg again, now). It was snowy and very cold (for Californians) but not as bad as we had feared. The hotels were ferociously hot and we soon had to discard our thermal underwear in favor of top layers which could be removed easily when we went indoors. Intourist provided us with S buses and guides so we got tours of the cities we visited, in between rehearsing, performing and being lionized and feted by the locals.

In Leningrad, we had been invited to sing at the Glinka Capella and also as part of the service celebrating the 1000th anniversary of the founding of the Russian Orthodox Church, at the huge, impressive Trinity Cathedral. Rachmaninoff's *Liturgy* had been banned by the Soviets at the time of the 1917 Revolution as being "too western" or "too modern" and had completely disappeared from concert repertoire or sacred services until it was found and resurrected by Tony. Some of the people who came to the Leningrad concerts remembered hearing it from 70 years earlier (or so they said)

The concert at the Glinka Capella was particularly emotional. The hall had 400 seats but 600 tickets had been sold, so there were Russians filling the aisles and entrances. We were being taped for Soviet radio and Tony was interviewed so the anticipation in the air was electric! By 7:30 pm the crowd began the rhythmic clapping which is done here and kept it up as we processed on stage. It was so thrilling. I and others were in tears by the time we took our places. Tony spoke to the crowd in Russian and he and Alex, the bass soloist who is of Russian descent, were allowed to sing the chants in the Liturgy which are usually reserved for priests. It was truly an historic event. Before we even started to sing, Tony received a bouquet of carnations from a local choir who wanted to show their appreciation of what we were doing.

The Liturgy lasts about an hour and went beautifully, considering how tired we all were. After the intermission we performed a Bach motet and four American spirituals and the crowd went wild again. More flowers and rhythmic clapping, two encores and people stood through all this to hear us. This was also the pattern for all our concerts in the other cities — Alushta (near the Ukraine), Kiev and Moscow — lack of sleep, exhaustion, below zero temperatures, unappetizing food, colds and coughs, but everywhere extravagant praise and thanks. Russians can be often very sentimental and emotional people. We were entertained with special dances and singing, were wined, dined, gifted and wept over everywhere we performed. Altogether more than 5000 people heard us sing their music in their language and heard our director, speaking their language, making explicit our message of friendship and peace.

In addition there were all the personal exchanges of good will that took place between the 189 of us Americans and the many Soviet people we each met. Several in our group could speak a little Russian and some were invited to private homes. There were plenty of social occasions before and after concerts, at the ballet and the circus, on the tours of local museums, cathedrals, historical monuments or in stores or eating and drinking spots for exchange of greetings and smiles and of small gifts such as pens, pins, and snapshots.

A Hostel Environment

To begin with, the hostel wasn't even in the right place. I hadn't looked at the guide book or the map carefully and we, my friend John and I, ended up forty miles of rough, winding road away from where we wanted to be. We finally located the sagging, two story log building on Highway 49 at the edge of East Glacier, Montana. It looked pleasant enough in spite of being rundown, with a screened front porch full of young people enjoying Happy Hour and a crowded snack bar and grocery store behind that, where we found the registration place at the checkout counter.

We were greeted by a very friendly, wiry, middle-aged man in shorts and tank top who introduced himself as Denis, the manager. He ushered us up the tilting, narrow stairs at the back of the store, which led to the living quarters, and warned John to duck his head so he wouldn't bump it as we emerged through a plywood trap door onto the second story. Denis told us that after this we should go up the outside stairs at the back of the building rather than through the store and snack bar. There was a sitting area with a few chairs in various stages of shedding their upholstery, a kitchen and beds for 25 hostelers — in two dorms and a few private rooms. I had reserved a private room with two beds for $23 a night but Denis said he had to go "check on it," so we sat in the lopsided chairs drank our beer and waited while young people speaking foreign languages plied the hall, dragging their duffles and backpacks.

Finally, Denis returned, very apologetic: the room with two beds had somehow gone to someone else and the best he could do was give us a futon. John insisted on sleeping on the floor; in spite of his feeling so poorly, and we hauled our bags up the high, wobbly back stairs and prepared to make the best of things.

Investigating the bathrooms, we found hand printed signs on the doors stating that the water had been found unsafe for drinking by the local health department. We could get bottled water in the kitchen. But when we went to get some, Denis told us that the water was really O.K. and not to worry about it. We talked to several fellow hostelers and opinion was divided as to the potability of the water. We chose to believe the Health Department and bought bottled water in the store (since the complimentary supply had been depleted and not replenished) but we had to remember to take water with us whenever we went to the bathroom to brush our teeth or take a pill. The women's bathroom consisted of a long counter with two sinks and two mirrors, a shower which leaked onto the floor, and two toilets which were almost impossible to get into or out of when anyone was at the sinks.

I had ten days worth of laundry to do and the Hostel Guide Book had advertised Laundry Facilities so I asked Denis where the machines were. He took me back down the front stairs and through the restaurant kitchen where he was in the midst of baking pies, to the washer by the back door: told me I could just unload the clothes in it, which he hadn't had time to do, and produced a split plastic basket so I could accomplish this.

I managed to get a large load done by about 7:30 and asked where the dryer was. Denis was up to his eyebrows in baking, registering new arrivals, taking money at the snack bar, getting toilet paper for the men's room and answering the phone. He never lost his smile but he explained he was shorthanded and he couldn't possibly take time to show me the dryer tonight. My clothes, he assured me, would dry overnight on the line in the warm, dry Montana air. All I had to do was remove the clothes that were now on the line and put them on the phone cable spools nearby. I was exhausted and very hungry and John was too ill to help, but I pulled the dry laundry off the line and bundled it up as smoothly as I could. It consisted of at least 20 sheets and pillow cases from the previous night's guests. I finally got my clothes, including 3 pairs of jeans and 8 pairs of heavy socks, hung out by a little after 8:00. The sun was still shining but I didn't have much confidence in its drying ability that late.

Finally, it was time to attack the supper problem. We had agreed to have, at the end of this long, hard day, a simple supper of a hearty canned soup, bread and butter, fruit and cookies. We carried our supplies up from the van in my daypack, forgetting only a few essential items, found the appropriate utensils in the kitchen and solved the mysteries of the unfamiliar stove, where someone had left a pot of water to boil, a pot which was now almost dry. I turned off the heat but before long a woman came rushing in, exclaimed, "Oh, did I forget that?" refilled the pan and turned on the heat, then rushed out again. We managed to get our soups heated and to sit down at the table when a group of six young people was ushered in by Denis' wife, Linda, who was taking a break from running her restaurant next door in order to give Denis a hand. She gave the new arrivals a long, shrill lecture about the rules of the kitchen, ending up by threatening them with being locked out of the kitchen if they didn't obey the rules. Unlike Denis, she never smiled. And she didn't say what we were supposed to do if the young people got us locked out of the kitchen. Mealtime ambience was deteriorating fast.

Just then, the woman with the boiling water came back in, this time laden with vegies and followed by a much younger man — a son? A lover? She apologized again for leaving the boiling water unattended and bustled around making her dinner preparations while chattering nonstop: Where were we from, where were we going, had we been to — — — , it had taken them 9 hours from Seattle, they were planning to bike over the Going to the Sun Highway, when had I lived in Berkeley, she'd lived there for a while, too. All perfectly friendly but by then we were too tired and uncomfortable to be very responsive, I fear. We gave her our unappetizing, leftover soup, washed our dishes in the doublecloroxed water, as prescribed, and retired to our room.

Our room was about 8 X 10 feet and there was just space, at the foot of the double bed, to spread John's futon on the floor and still open up the door far enough to squeeze through. In order to go to the bathroom, which I have to do at least twice every night, I had to carefully step over John's 6 ft. 5 in. length, unhook the door and open it just far enough for me to slide through into the hail, then pull the door to and hook it on the outside so it wouldn't swing open again, bumping into sleeping John and exposing him to the people tramping back and forth in the hall. Of course, that meant John was trapped in the bedroom for the length of time I was in the bathroom, but luckily he did not wake up and discover this.

It was still only 10:00 o'clock when John went to bed and I was hoping to find lodging for the next 3 nights in St. Mary, the town I had thought the hostel was in and the place we wanted to be because it was much closer to the hikes we planned to take. So I walked along the deserted highway about two blocks to the nearest pay phone. Of course, the phone book was missing and the phone ate all my quarters without getting me through to Directory Assistance. I gave up in defeat and decided we would just try to get used to conditions at the hostel and to driving an extra hour every day to the trail heads.

We both slept poorly because of all the noise in the hall and John woke up with such a pain in his gut that I was afraid I would have to take him to the Emergency Room of the Indian Hospital, 50 miles away in Browning, on the Rez. We were told the Indians there were not very kind to Whites but there was no place else to go. Luckily, he felt better after tea and a muffin in the snack bar, which I talked him into having while I rearranged my jeans and socks on the clothesline to take advantage of the morning sun. We had to be out of the hostel by 9:00 A.M. and, by now, we had agreed that we wanted to leave for good, even though finding a place to stay, or even camp, in Glacier Park on a Friday night was a pretty risky undertaking.

Two hours later we had a very comfortable place to stay, for more than three times the cost of the hostel, at the big Inn and Resort in St. Mary and my clothes had finished drying in the back of the van. John recovered in a day or two and I learned that I am probably too old for Youth Hostels. When an impersonal Motel 6 looks like a warm haven to me, I know I am too old.

A Spiritual Autobiography

In my childhood, religion was never discussed in my home and I had almost no spiritual guidance as I was growing up. My father was an ex-Lutheran agnostic, my mother a lapsed Quaker and my grandmother, though she still went to Friends' Meeting sometimes and practiced their principles, taught me more by example than by lecturing. My parents were married by a Unitarian minister, as well as in a Quaker ceremony, and the family did attend the Unitarian Church occasionally, where my grandmother was active in the Women's Alliance as a social activity. I went to Unitarian Sunday School because my friends went there and it was within walking distance of my home, but I can remember nothing I learned there. My grandmother had read me Van Loon's *Stories from the Bible* so I was at least familiar with the cast of characters. And I had seen plenty of depictions of God and all the other religious figures in paintings and had heard what my more orthodox friends were supposed to believe.

I remember very clearly when I decided to reject all the stories and pictures as nonsense. I was twelve years old and had prayed to God for weeks to keep me from throwing up after some surgery I had to have. But I threw up prodigiously, in spite of my prayers. When I got back home, I looked at myself in the mirror and said to myself "What a ridiculous story! There is no old man with a white beard up in the sky who watches over people." After that I had no God but I still went

OVERCOMING CHILDHOOD ADVANTAGES

to Unitarian young people's group. It saved my life in High School where I was younger than everyone else and socially retarded besides. I learned to look and behave like a fairly normal teenager while I dreamed of finding the perfect, once in a lifetime, forever and ever love. I had read a lot of fairy stories and romantic tales and my search for True Love really served as a sort of religious quest in those years. The rest of my life, at that time, was consumed by striving for academic excellence and peer acceptance. I don't think I had any real-life heroes or heroines then. But I had a sort of composite ideal woman I wanted to be like — a beautiful, gentle, calm, nurturing, intelligent, funny, wise, sexy, well-loved woman, simple and sincere — a sort of junior Earth Mother. In reality, I was a lonely, uptight, overly serious, adult-dominated teenager with a good figure but an unfortunate case of acne (which increased my feelings of inferiority and isolation).

I was a college freshman, just sixteen, when I met Ed, who became my first and most important mentor. He was seven years older and seemed to know everything. We were singing together in the University Chorus — music so beautiful and thrilling, like the Mozart Requiem, that I believe it was my first "spiritual" experience. Often the music was liturgical but the words didn't bother me; I didn't have to believe them and they were usually in Latin or German, anyway. It took me two years of pursuing Ed to catch him and two more before we were married. During all that time in college, music and love sustained my soul.

After graduation and marriage, I had to leave music — at least choral singing — to be an Army bride, but now I devoted myself to nurturing my "perfect" love and to becoming the "perfect" wife and mother. Sexual ecstasy was, to me, a transcendent, hence spiritual, experience. The births of my children were also sublime, peak experiences, although the pain and fear of the first delivery kept me from appreciating that one until afterwards. Meanwhile, my life rolled and bumped along the mostly routine track of raising the children, growing in my relationship to Ed, adjusting to his job moves and trying to get along on very little money. I don't think I was spending much time on — or even aware of — spiritual matters during those years.

Finally, I grew tired of being so broke and went to work and to school again, so I could get a better job. After quite a few years of jobs I didn't like and classes I found deadly, I was able to get a job which gave me a lot of satisfaction and independence. I don't think my feelings about it were spiritual but they were certainly ego enhancing. For the first time I felt I was really helping people outside my family and friends and that feeling is food for the soul. My life during these busy years was not entirely without contemplation or reflection but I was not looking for answers to anything I thought of as "spiritual". Instead, I had turned to psychology for a better understanding of myself and those around me. I went to a shrink, I read some Freud and Jung and others, and I engaged in small bull sessions with psychologist friends and with Ed — the kind of searching most people work their way through in college but which I had ignored in favor of Science and Love.

I thought my life was going along quite well when suddenly it all fell apart. Ed was in love with another woman whom he had been seeing secretly for six months. I didn't want a divorce and was determined to win him back. He didn't want a divorce — he just wanted both of us — but he was willing to get marriage counseling, in fact, suggested it himself. We tried some local therapists without feeling that they were helping any, then decided to try Esalen which then, in 1969, was just becoming trendy. Thus began a period in my life during which Esalen was, in effect, my religion. We went there many times and experienced many of its methods: a lot of heavy Gestalt work, dream work, bioenergetics, Tai Chi, art therapy, naked massage, psychodrama, guided fantasy, meditation, sensory awareness, group process, creative movement — the whole bag. The hot baths and a little marijuana helped, too, and I would return from a stay at Esalen on a real spiritual high. Mostly, we went as a couple and worked on our relationship but sometimes we went separately and worked only on ourselves. Our experiences there saved our marriage and made profound and lasting changes in our lives. They gave us tools to deal with future problems.

After a few years of this mellowing out and loosening up, Ed decided to get out of Bureaucracy at age fifty-five and devote himself to being a lovable and wise Village Blacksmith, demonstrating turn of the century ironworking at various State and National Parks. I kept working for three more years but Ed seemed to be having all the fun and, also, my parents were needing a lot of help at this time in their lives. So I quit work at age fifty-one. I've never been sorry, but then there was no money for Esalen or much of anything else. We moved to Point Reyes, where Ed was blacksmithing, and suddenly I had much too much time on my hands as the children were all on their own by now. Ed and I tried a little backpacking and though he soon gave it up because of a bad foot, I got hooked and kept on with it as well as with day hiking long, solitary miles all over the Point Reyes Peninsula, The hiking became a moving meditation for me and being out in the natural world stimulated my awareness of my spiritual connection to it. My confidence in my ability to take care of myself increased greatly and the beauty and grandeur of the seashore and mountains, and of the less dramatic places in between, always gave my spirit a lift.

I had taken up weaving about the time Ed took up blacksmithing and now I had plenty of time for it — exploring a creativity I never thought I had — and for making something beautiful and useful completely on my own. I also discovered that weaving can be a meditation much like walking: the rhythm, the forward progress that comes step-by-step or row-by-row, the suspension of worrisome thoughts — even the sense of achievement at the end. Ed was getting itchy, though, and we moved again, this time to Santa Cruz. It was a hard time for me, my father had recently been killed by a car and my mother required full time nursing care — did not even recognize me. She remained a vegetable for three years until she died and I had to do a lot of hard thinking about dying and how I wanted to die. I could see nothing "spiritual" about the way either of my parents died and grew impatient with all the Death Experts who were writing about how beautiful and uplifting Death is.

Meanwhile, I continued to work on discovering and improving myself and my relationship with Ed. We were both enjoying the arrival of grandchildren, the opportunity to travel together and to get back into singing together again. All these experiences and explorations had a spiritual component for me. I did a lot of traveling and camping and hiking by myself, too, as Ed wasn't crazy about camping and couldn't hike far. I really tested myself, with up to six weeks of solitary exploration, all around the Western States and later in Canada. High in the Rockies or deep in Utah's Canyonlands. I felt pretty spiritual — even when I was scared. (These days, people pay a lot of money to be led on such a Vision Quest.)

In the interests of self-improvement and for handling problems as they arose, Ed and I continued to belong to an ongoing therapy group. The therapist was a good friend who gave us a cut rate or let us come free just because he thought we contributed to the group. Sometimes we went separately and sometimes together and we always got a lot of support from the group. A big group hug or laying on of hands can feel pretty spiritual. There were more marital problems which previous experience and group understanding helped us to solve. Ed had spells when he wanted to have both me and a mistress and I wasn't happy with that! But we had a deep underlying devotion to and respect for each other and working through this problem really, made our relationship stronger and, eventually, serene and happy.

About this time, the question of "What is Spirituality?" came up at the Unitarian Fellowship where Ed and I were active. The members of the congregation wanted the Fellowship to give them more of it but nobody could define what it was. I had never really thought about it before and now I was forced to consider what this slippery word meant to me. All the experiences which I have described as "spiritual" in this story I have labeled thus only in retrospect. My spirit is nourished by nature, by music, by making love, by family and friends, by any kind of peak experience. I do not feel this way in church; the Fellowship is my community, my support group of kindred souls.

At that same time my younger daughter and the man who is now her second husband were getting deep into New Age mysticism and trying to educate me in their ways. They claimed to be seekers of Spiritual Truth and challenged me to join them. I was already doing Yoga stretching and breathing, some trancing or self hypnosis, occasionally acupuncture or massage or herbal remedies but I used these techniques for physical well being and stress reduction. I could not get myself to believe in the theories behind the practices. Nor was I sold on shamans, witches, goddess worship, the importance of past lives or the power of the I Ching, Tarot cards, Ouija boards or crystal pendulums in helping make life decisions. Apparently, my early scientific training is too strongly a part of me for me to be able to accept these dimensions of spirituality (if that is what they are), All these symbols, rituals, and worship figures are, to me, not that different from those found in orthodox religions. I worship the natural world, love, family, music, friendships — not necessarily in that order.

Ed and I were in a very good place, feeling easy with each other and happy with our lives, making plans for our future, when he died so suddenly. It was as if I had been dropped into a deep black pit. All my adult life, he was my main source of emotional support. Even when he was fooling around, he did not stop loving me, nor I him, though I got very angry at him sometimes. Gradually, I have been learning how to be single, how to live without that wonderful security of loving and being loved. Though I do not have a loving mate or belief system to sustain me spiritually, I do have the marvels of nature, the glory of music, the excitement of discovering new people, places and things, the warmth of friends and the fascinating (to me) unfolding of my children's and grandchildren's lives. All these mysteries of my life are my soul food.

www.ingramcontent.com/pod-product-compliance
Lightning Source LLC
Chambersburg PA
CBHW030308080526
44584CB00012B/486